Dedicated to all my nieces-

Clarissa, Lisa, Stephanie, Sonya,

Michelle, Kristen, Victoria, Rosa and so many more.

Bad Auntie

What Momma Won't Tell You Auntie Will

by Rose M. Gore

ISBN: 1441494499

Contact information for requests for permission to reproduce or distribute materials is listed below:

badauntie@yahoo.com

www.myspace.com/bad_auntie

Magnificent Images
PO Box 10545
Erie PA 16514

Table of Contents

Introduction

When a woman reaches thirty, there is an odor that develops and emanates from a part of her anatomy like no other. It's a chicken soup like odor that… well; we'll get into that later. The point is why didn't Momma tell me about this when I was younger?

I believe that Aunties have a great responsibility to their nieces and nephews and I am the world's greatest Auntie just ask my many nieces or nephews.

There is nothing that I would not do for them. I keep their secrets, I give them money, I've taken them in off the streets even when their Mommas put them out and I make myself available to them "twenty-four, seven." When they cry I dry their tears and when stressed I relieve their fears. I'm the one they can talk to when they can't go to Momma.

Now don't get things tangled. I'm not trying to think myself to be more than a mother. That's crazy. I'm just saying we, the Aunties of the world, we have our place and no one can take it.

I do have to confess. I got nicknamed Bad Auntie for a reason. So what! I gave make-up to some of my nieces before they were allowed to wear it. I let them wear their hair down when they came over my house when their mothers didn't allow it. I snuck money to my nephews when I was told not to. I threw momma's breakfast out and fried my babies chicken. Oatmeal became oatmeal cookies (I mean what's the difference except for a little flour and baking powder) and veggies got tossed on a pizza. But this is just what good old Bad Aunties do. We listen, we talk out of turn and we tell you the things that Momma won't tell you.

Chapter 1

Momma Says

This book is mostly directed to the relationship between an auntie and her niece but everyone who reads it will enjoy and benefit from it.

So, let's keep it traditional ok ladies? We know that there're all kinds of moms out there but this chapter is about the average mom. You know the traditional mom, the mother that raised us to be responsible, respectable young ladies, yeah her. The one that says you can be anything you want to be, a doctor a lawyer or an um, um… an engineer, yeah.

Anyway the real moms, the ones who say, keep your head up and your dress down, your eyes open and your leg closed. Not the ones who say "make that money". Now that I've got that established lets move on.

I give honor to my mother for she is the greatest mom ever to live. She did indeed teach my sister and me how to be ladies, feminine, all around women. I really love her for that but let's face it there's some things momma just didn't tell me.

Right away when I say "what Momma won't tell you Auntie will" most people think of sex but in this day and time most mothers talk to their daughters about sex. Nawl, I'm talking about more things, big things that seem to be little things that mom just didn't think to tell you. I do touch on some things of a sexual nature because some subjects daughters are just not really comfortable talking about with mom and vice versa. Now mommies, don't get mad but I don't care how open you are with your daughters about sex there're some things she's just not going to share with you…but she will tell me. Now again, you may have had one of those free loving mommas that told you everything that you thought you wanted to know but I didn't.

Momma, she means well but let's face it her job is to tell us right from wrong. She'll say things like, baby if God wanted you to have blond hair he would have given it to you. Auntie will tell you girl, you should have been born a blonde. Momma says there's nothing wrong with your eyebrows. I say, pluck that bush.

Mommies love their babies. She'll say, "Just be yourself and everyone will love you." I call this "The Big Fib." This is the lie you'll hear from so many people, teachers, councilors, talk show host and even dudes.

Guys say, "I like a girl to just be herself." Yeah right! He's lying to you. The only time a guy wants you to be yourself is when you're already what he wants in a woman. Auntie says what? That's right. "Fake it till you make it" or more like "trick um till you get um." *Bwaaaaaaah!* Seriously, most of us have heard from older women (mommas) that what it took to get him it'll take the same thing to keep him. Unfortunately that's true. I'm sorry to say it but men don't change so we have too. You're going to fight me on this but it's still the truth. Now you really don't have to change. You can have one of those "yes men" or you can keep changing boyfriends like you change your panties. But the truth is, to get and keep the man you want you're going to have to make some adjustments. So the trick is to not become someone that you yourself can't live with. After all, we're looking for happiness. You should do everything you can to make your mate happy unless it makes you unhappy.

Now most Mommas are Aunties too. The thing is they deal with their daughters differently from the way they deal with their nieces. My Aunties told me a lot of things that they never told their daughters. So just like daughters can't go to their mothers with everything mothers can't confide everything to their daughters. When they do they risk what we call "getting too familiar" with them and this may cause problems in the relationship. The mother daughter relationship becomes blurred and it becomes more like a sister to sister relationship. If you try to be your child's friend more than her mother you will pay for it in the future. You will lose the respect due you and have only the respect afforded a friend. Now if that's all you want then I say rock on but don't be mad when they give more respect to the next door neighbor than they do you.

...and moving right along.

Chapter 2

Grandma Says

Good Ol'grandma. Again I had the best. At the time of this writing I do still have one living Grandmother and she'll be 100 years old Lord willing on March 11, 2009 and oh my, what a treasure. I draw great wisdom from her.

Good Grandmas, (and please don't ask me what a good grandma is) will sometimes tell you what momma won't but she'll put a whole different spin on it than an Auntie will. She is quite direct and to the point, sometimes crass and shockingly blunt but her wisdom is un-compared. One thing that Aunties and Grandmas have in common is they will tell you things you don't want to know. So unless you really want to know, don't ask.

Now, grandmothers vary depending on the generation in which they were born. But they're basically the same especially the good ol'fashion ones.

Grandmothers from my generation will tell you "Know your place. Let that man be right." But I say, "Wrong is just wrong." Now from time to time it may seem like I'm contradicting myself but that just means you're not paying close enough attention.

Letting that man be right is good up to a point. If he says carrots are better for you than spinach, you know it's not true. Don't say no it's not. Just say something like carrots are really good for you. So when do we disagree? When he says, baby hand me the gasoline to light the charcoal, we're out of lighter fluid and they're the same thing. That's when you speak up and say NO! They're not the same thing. You can sit back and say nothing if you want but you'll be dining on the delicate taste of gasoline soaked chicken. That is of course if he doesn't burn the house down first. There is a time to speak up and a time to shut up. It takes practice I know and it's going to take a while for some of you to get the hang of it but the reason I'm telling you is so you'll be aware of it and you can't say you didn't know. You see that's what Aunties do. We remove your excuses so you can't say that you didn't know better.

Grandmothers are great! They have a wealth of experience and knowledge. As a matter of fact Grandmothers will talk to their grand-daughters much like an aunt will but a lot of their solutions to your problems may be a little out dated. Never dismiss anything they tell you because if you listen closely their answers can almost always be updated and adapted.

Chapter 3

Auntie Says

So, now we come to it…Aunties. I am an Auntie in its purest form. I have no children. So I'm nobody's mother or grandmother. I'm just an Auntie, a real Auntie. Most of my nieces and nephews will tell you that I'm their favorite Auntie.

Being an Auntie is a job and I take my job seriously. If my babies ask me for something and I can't give it to them it hurts me. If they ask me a question and I can't answer it that disturbs me. Being a pure Auntie is so different from being a regular Auntie. Nieces and nephews are more likely to come to us with their problems and secrets. So please Aunties don't betray their trust. If they come to you with a serious issue that you think they should tell their mother encourage them to do so. DON"T do it for them. If it's a life threatening situation insist that they go to their mother even if you have to go with them. But only when you can't convince them to talk to their parents and only in the most serious situations do you betray their trust.

My nieces and nephews have come to me with everything from how to get the greasy build up out of their hair to should they leave their no good lying cheating nigg…I mean um, um man.

Being a good Auntie is an enormous responsibility. You must be able to advise your nieces and nephews on everything even if you don't have any experience in the particular situation.

They are not always comfortable going to the people who may have the experience so Aunties must be prepared. If we lack experience in a situation we rely on common sense, wisdom and the things our mothers and grandmothers did tell us, not to mention the things our "Bad Aunties" told us. The good thing is we don't have to hold back. As where sometimes Mommies are a little shy about saying things, Auntie's aren't. I can't begin to tell you all the things that my nieces have asked me over the years so I'll just touch on a few. Let's start with hygiene, yep, yep.

Hygiene, now why would Auntie have to tell you anything about hygiene? This is a subject that our Mommies cover thoroughly right? Well, I don't know but my nieces have called me from time to time with a question or two. I think sometimes Mommies take for granted that daughters know things that they don't and there're some things that our mothers just neglect to tell us for whatever reason. Then, there're things that she just assumes you'll figure out. Take for instance, when a woman reaches thirty, there is an odor that develops and emanates from between her breast like no other. This chicken soup like odor can nearly render you incapacitated. When this phenomenon first occurs, you might spend hours trying to figure out just where the odor's coming from.

A friend of mine told me that she smelled a strange odor one day but she couldn't figure out where it was coming from. She knew that it was coming from her body but she still couldn't figure out what part. She checked up under her arms and that wasn't it. She did the breath test (For those of you who don't know how to administer the breath test, lift your right hand. Place said hand one half inch in front of your mouth and say harrrrr, sniffing quickly.) When she realized it wasn't her breath the woman went to the ladies room to check down below. *(Y'all like how I put that "Down beeeelow.)* When she realized that it wasn't coming from that part of her body she was stumped, so she went back to her office. The odor continued to follow her until…Nooooooo! Could it be? She inserted two fingers down between her breasts and brought them back up to her nose. Yep, chicken soup!

I remember when I first discovered the odor. I told my Mom about it and she broke out laughing. I asked her, why had she not told me about this? She said, "Because I never thought about it." Then we both laughed. This was probably the pivotal moment I realized I had to write this book, "What Momma won't tell."

I am so tired of women walking around smelling like chicken soup, clean women too! I'm talking about women that handle their business, take baths, deodorize, lotion, powder, perfume their bodies and yet they still smell like chicken soup. You see they haven't figured out where the odor is coming from or they have and just don't know what to do about it. I don't care how large or small your breasts are you are not immune to this problem. So what's the solution? It's simple. Place a small cotton cloth or ladies handkerchief between your breasts. Yep! That's it. If you're not sensitive, scent the fabric first with your cologne of the day.

Back in the nineteen forties and fifties women wore scented hankies between their breast as evident in the old black and white movies. I thought it was done to be sexy. But I found out later …the hard way, the real reason.

Some women say powder works just as well but I beg to differ. I love powder but powder has to be reapplied throughout the day and this of course could get messy. I recommend the hankie. It keeps you smelling fresh and sweet all day long.

Odors seem to take on a life of their own. It's like they're these little creatures hiding somewhere on your body just to embarrass you. So just in case some of you out there didn't have a Bad Auntie I want to tell you some of the little buggers hiding places.

Let's start with your clitoris or "clit" as some of you like to call it. You will be surprised how many women wash their genital area and ignore their clit. Some women spend money unnecessarily on yeast infection products thinking they have a yeast infection when they just need to pay more attention to cleaning their clit. Without proper and thorough attention bacteria can set up causing problems including serious odor. So please, clean between the cracks and crevices.

And speaking of cracks, have you ever been seated next to someone that had on a nice fragrant perfume and smelled really good, that is until they stood up? Upon standing they released an odor that a skunk would be proud of. You said to yourself where did that come from? I'll tell you where, they were sitting on it!

One day I went to the post office and as I was getting my mail together a woman passed by me. She smelled so good that I turned around to ask her what she was wearing. I said wow! You really smell good. What are you wearing?

The woman gleefully divulged.

As she turned to walk away I got a whiff of a different fragrance that wasn't so pleasant. Then I saw the astonished look on the faces of the people that filled the lobby. I was so embarrassed knowing that they thought I loved the smell of boo-boo.

Now I know that y'all think that I'm going to say wash your "A" (A stands for appendage because y'all know I don't cuss). Wrong, everybody knows that. But what some don't understand is you have to dry it!

A lot of people don't know to dry off completely especially in and under the folds of your body. The larger the body, the more the folds, the more time you need to take drying off. Of the fat people who do smell, a lot of them smell not because they didn't bathe but because they didn't take the time out to dry off thoroughly. You see if you're already wet you just give sweat a head start on making you stink.

Other places odors love to hide that most people ignore are around the nose, the crease of the thigh, under your hanging stomach and behind your knees. We all should know about the crease of the thigh and under our hanging stomachs but I mentioned it just incase. The solution to this is the above mentioned. Dry off totally! Some people like to air dry and that's okay for the most part. But remember the air can't dry what the air can't get to. If you have folds and rolls you have to dry off in between them and a little powder here won't hurt.

A lot of us don't know about the nose odor and the odor behind the knees. Now I'm not saying that everybody has it, we all have our own body chemistry. But there's a simple test that you can administer to check. Just slide your finger along the side of your nose pressing firmly then smell your finger. It will tell the story, (said test works equally as well behind the knee). So ladies it's simple, just dry off…dudes you too!

Another problem some women face is excessive vaginal discharge. Of course you should always go to your doctor for regular exams to make sure there's not a medical problem. Once you know that is not medical what do you do? I always advise you to wear panty-liners and change them as often as necessary. I can't stress enough how important it is to stay dry. And ladies, please, please stop douching unless you take more showers than baths. If you're one of the girls who prefer showers then I'll let you be the judge but women who take baths rarely need to douche.

I had an Auntie who used to advise young women about hygiene. One young lady told her about a vaginal odor that she just couldn't get rid of no matter how hard she tried. My Aunt, *God rest her soul*, told the group of ladies that sometimes you might have to put a little bleach in your bathwater. Waaaaaaah! I laughed so hard when she told me that.

Now ladies I can't recommend bleach but one thing I know works is white vinegar. Pour a generous amount of white vinegar in your bathwater and take a nice soak. I know what you're thinking. How could something so smelly make you smell fresh? Vinegar is just great for getting rid of strong odors. You know that sometimes it takes fire to fight fire. Vinegar is great for mopping your floors, getting sour smells out of carpet and clothing and a streak free window cleaner. Try it. It really works! It also makes a really good hair rinse.

Now, to me there is nothing more important than good hygiene but did you know that some men like musty women? It's the truth. I didn't believe it but it is true. A lot of women have told me stories of their husband or boyfriends cheating on them with women who were nasty, stinking, dirty, musty and just an all around mess. These are the women who walk by you when your back is turned and you don't hear them but boy do you smell them. You turn around to see what passed by and you can't believe it was human let alone a woman. Yet some men seem to love theses what I call D-frees. D-frees' are people who don't believe in deodorizing or perfuming their bodies. They do not believe in wearing any type of deodorant or perfume. My friend told me of a lady who was a devout d-free. She would go to the club in the summertime dressed beautifully but musty as could be. Then she would dance up a storm making her stench even more fragrant. Everyone talked about her like a dog behind her back and she knew it but this did not bother her. One day she told my friend, I know I'm musty but men like it like that. Oh they talk about me, she said but when no ones looking they go home with me. My friend responded in shock. Really, why do you think they like you musty? Her explanation was that men love the natural scent of a woman. She said the scent of a woman's "poontang" arouses them and if they can smell your "poontang" they will follow you home. Come to find out that she had been with most of the guys that hung out at that club and a vast number of men through out the city. Now I don't know if there's any truth to her theory because I'm just not willing to test it. But I must say almost every woman I know say men seem to get clingier when they are menstruating.

Now let's talk about bleach. I may not have enough nerve to put it in my bath but I have used it on my skin with caution.

Working as a preschool teacher can be hazardous to your health. You can go to work alone and come home with so many little friends. I'm not talking about the children either. I'm talking about them blasted ringworms. They're so easy to get but so hard to get rid of.

One of my nieces moved in with me with her baby. Her child was enrolled in daycare and came home one day with ringworms. Being the conscientious mother that she was she immediately took her child to the doctor. Her physician prescribed a cream that was supposed to take care of the problem. It didn't. Days went by, weeks went by and the baby still had ringworm. Frustrated she asked me, "Auntie what should I do?" Reluctantly I told her to get the bleach. I know I know. I can just hear y'all screaming. But it works. I told her to get a Q-tip, dip it in bleach and apply it to the infected area then wipe with clear water. She did that for a couple of days and the ringworms were gone. The prescribed tube of cream went to the trash. Now any doctor would probably try to have you arrested for doing this so it's your decision. I just tell my nieces what works.

There are some things that you should have in the house at all times. Bleach of course is very important. Along with bleach there is vinegar, baking soda, peroxide, petroleum jelly (Vaseline), alcohol, (that's rubbing alcohol people) and a good first aid kit. These are inexpensive things that come in handy in a pinch.

Bleach can be used to disinfect when you run out of cleaners and adding just a little bit to your dish water can cut the grease, kill stubborn germs and remove those awful spaghetti sauce stains from your favorite plastic ware.

Baking soda I can't live without. It does everything from freshening up the refrigerator to whitening up your teeth. Backing soda can also be used in your bath water to give you a fresh feeling.

Baking soda and vinegar will keep your drains open and clog free. I had a stubborn drain in my bathroom that I had to unclog every time I look around. I used every drain opener on the market and I plunged and plunged and plunged but it would soon clog up again. One day I decided to try the baking soda and vinegar and it worked. After plunging my drain I put two tablespoons of baking soda in the drain followed by a cup of vinegar. The bathroom drain never clogged up again. Did you hear me say never? It's been years and it still runs free.

Peroxide is another must have. It can do everything from disinfecting a wound to freshening up bad breath. When mixed with baking soda it becomes a nice teeth whitening toothpaste. Peroxide works like magic in getting blood out. Pour it on a blood stain and watch it disappear. I've even used it on old set-in blood stains.

Vaseline or petroleum jelly is like gooey gold. It can be used for anything from protecting your skin to protecting your leather shoes. It is the grease I use in my hair and it is the least expensive and most effective way there is to clear up a rash. It is my head to toe remedy. Some black women don't believe in greasing their scalps so I say to you, "you do you." But to my fellow sisters who still believe in the grease, a jar of petroleum jelly from the dollar store can come in handy in a pinch. I use petroleum jelly instead of the over priced, over advertised, over rated hair dressing products. And if you look at the first ingredient in most hair grease products you'll probably see what, petroleum jelly.

Beautiful skin is so important and I don't know about you but I refuse to pay for the high price skin care products on the market today. Most of them are again over-rated much like those fancy hair care products that promise to grow you long luxurious hair (y'all stop spending your money on that mess).

I love Vaseline. I do. I do. I do. It heals my rashes, scratches and scrapes and protects my skin as well.

From time to time I will break out in some random rash on my face and all I do is generously cover my face in Vaseline over night. The next morning the rash is gone, my skin is baby butt smooth and I'm back to my beautiful self. Now don't confuse a rash with bumps. Most bumps are caused by acne and calls for more drastic measures. Maybe bleach …bwaaaaaaah, just kidding, hummmmmmm or am I?

Some ladies put a little Vaseline on their teeth to prevent lipstick from getting on them and I know a lot of women who only use Vaseline as their lip gloss. If you live in a cold climate i.e. Erie PA then lotion doesn't work in the winter. You go to work or school moisturized and half way through the day you're ashy. That is not a good look. Appling Vaseline over your lotion will solve this problem. And ladies please don't forget the feet especially your crusty heels. You may need to pumice them first. Vaseline can work wonders but not miracles.

Now for the critics, to the ones who say Vaseline clogs the scalp and leaves a build up. Just wash your hair in a good dish detergent from time to time you'll have no problem. And if they tell you it'll clog your pores, just use a good skin toner and you'll stay refreshed. The non-secret is to keep your skin clean, moisturized, and protected and it will keep you beautiful.

So, you can take my advice and helpful hints or ignore them. You say it's a good read and maybe a little funny but my life is just fine and these little things won't change anything. But do you ever wonder why Nancy Normal is doing so much better than you for no good reason. You're the same age, you have the same educational background, you're both attractive and outgoing and yet she seems to always get ahead. It's because Nancy Normal does all the extra little things that you say doesn't matter.

So from now on listen to what your "Bad Auntie" tells you. I still listen to mine and they are truly wise.

I give honor to them; Aunt Sister, Aunt Carrie, Auntie (Aunt Mae Lee), Aunt Vick, Aunt Mary Ann and my Aunt May. Smooches!

Chapter 4

A Woman's Body

A woman's body is a beautiful, intricate, complicated work of art. Our bodies go through more changes than Michael's face. I'm talking about breast development, menstruation, pregnancy, weight gain, weight loss, menopause and weight gain again. It's enough to give us constant nightmares. Oh and did I mention weight gain?

Being fat can be hell. I mean HELL! Yes, again I'm an expert. I have been overweight my entire life and have managed to get through it intact. This is largely accredited to my confidence and my high self-esteem. You see I have the kind of self-esteem that Mo'nique would be proud of and I once toppled the scale at 415lb. Okay! No one laughed at me (to my face) and people treated me great. Yes I've gotten the typical stares and glares but a lot of times it was because people were surprised to see a person my size so dressed to impress, confidant and secure. After I busted them staring at me they usually say something like, I'm sorry I didn't mean to stare at you but you look beautiful. Yes, I get this response from both women and men.

One day I got dressed for a doctor's appointment, looked in the mirror and was pleased with what I saw. As I entered the office the receptionist said "Wow you look beautiful." Flattered I smiled and thanked her. At about 325lb this was truly a compliment. As I took my seat in the waiting room a receptionist from another office entered the room, gasped and said “oh my God I love your outfit, that’s sharp.” Thank you I said this time more bashfully. The next lady that entered the room walked by then backed up. “Girl that’s bad” she said looking at my outfit. Thank you I said this time embarrassingly as the whole waiting room full of people was now staring. A little while later a woman from the down stairs office came in the room and said I heard about you and I just came to see. Then I just covered my face as the whole room of patients continued to stare. Feeling great about the flattering compliment I was still relieved when my appointment was finished. As I was getting off the elevator a young man was getting on, he took a double take and said “Wow you look beautiful.”

So many fat women, (yes that’s what we are fat), will not dress-up because they say that they’ll still be fat. I say to them…………..STOP IT. Just stop it! If you want to lose weight try slowly changing your eating habits and never give up and realize that it’s easier to diet when you look good.

I am and always have been fat. I am and always was popular. I am and always will be cute. See, confidant right? Yet and still, I do not want my nieces to be fat. And being fat is not what I want to be. It is unhealthy and honestly it’s just not my favorite look. I’ve managed to lose a good bit of weight, no Weight Watchers no Jenny Craig or surgery just old fashion calories cutting. I’m very proud of myself but I still have a ways to go. I would love to be a size twelve. That would be perfect to me.

Does size matter? Well, let's just say it definitely shapes who you are and what you can and cannot do comfortably. There're some very healthy large size people who suffer no significant health issues but they face the same social and economical issues that the unhealthy face. A fat person can tell you of the nightmares of flying. I declare airplane seats were built for baby doll like creatures with no breast and no butt. My legs undergo awful bruising from the tight squeeze of the airplane seat and no matter how high your self esteem it is still embarrassing when you go to public places i.e....doctor's offices, amusement parks, restaurants, churches etc... and you can't fit into the seating. It's embarrassing to have to ask the airline attendant for a seatbelt extender or to have to wait for table seating at a restaurant because all they have available is booths and of course you don't fit.

Being overweight can be a problem. The price of wide shoes and plus size clothing are ridiculously higher than so called regular sizes. I hate to tell you how much plus size underwear cost but a hint, my bra order and my car note were the same.

Fashionable clothing are a little easier to find now than when I was a teenager but most plus size clothing are fashioned to suit your grandmother. Yet and still there are ways around these problems. I learned to sew at an early age and I really kept up with the "Jones". I got bigger and bigger but it was not a problem because I could always make something to fit. I prided myself on how I could beat the skinny chicks dressing. The thing I didn't think much about was my health. I walked six miles a day so I was in pretty good physical condition in spite of weight. My blood pressure was great and my cholesterol was excellent. I never worried about my weight gain because I figured that I could lose it whenever I wanted too. As I continued to gain weight the health problems seem to come on all at once. It seemed over night I wasn't able to walk the six miles a day that I had did everyday from age fourteen. All of a sudden I had high blood pressure and my cholesterol was high. I declare it all happened overnight but no it was the years of neglecting my health. I didn't too much care that I was fat so I just piled it on.

I'm from Erie, Pennsylvania, a city known for its snowy winters. After a heavy snow fall the snowplow would go through out the city removing the snow from the road. As they plowed the streets the snow would be pushed against the curb blocking driveways and walkways. A lot of times the only way to get from the street to your house was to climb over the snow banks. As I continued to pile on the weight I noticed that my feet would go deeper and deeper into the snow bank when I would have to climb over one so I learned to only climb over snow that contained ice or had hardened. I knew to test the snow first before stepping onto it. As I continued to get larger even the hardened snow began to give way under my weight until one day I sunk down half way through. Oh God! I was so embarrassed. I had the nerve to have had on high heels and when I did manage to get out, my shoes stayed in. Until this day I don't know how I got out of that hole I just know I did it quickly because I was so embarrassed. I didn't call for help because I didn't want anybody to see me stuck in the snow. The crazy thing is my feet didn't even get cold because I was too embarrassed to notice or care.

Now listen all nieces of the world, you can get so fat you can't reach to wipe you're "A" (A stands for anus, because y'all know I don't cuss). And if that's not enough you'll hate the way you look nude. Being celibate I didn't really worry about this much either. Again I figured that I could lose the weight when I found Mr. Right and be cute and dainty. I never realized that once you reach a certain weight you stretch your skin to a point of no return. Even if you lose the weight you'll still have the skin hanging. That is not a good look.

I used to see obese women with short pants on walking down the street. It wasn't really the short pants that looked so bad to me but it was the fat hanging behind their knees. Oh I thought it was so disgusting I just wanted them to put a skirt on and a long one at that. I think fat women are just as beautiful as thin women but some things are just unattractive and that fat hanging behind the knees is so ugly. Please, to my young ladies don't let your body get so stretched out of shape that it'll take life threatening surgery to get the loose skin removed.

A lot of the time surgery doesn't fix the problem. Surgery leaves scarring and that also is sooooooo not cute. They say you should love the skin you're in but it's hard when that skin is loose and hanging all over your body. Please I beg all young women don't let this happen to you. Get help when you see that your weight is out of control. Go on a diet or let your doctor put you on a diet. It's going to be hard but take your time. I feel the key to a successful diet is to go slow, slow, slow. After all it's better to lose twelve pounds a year (one pound a month) than to never lose a pound because you keep putting it off until you're ready.

One day I was walking downtown Erie PA and I felt a strange presence on my back. As I continued to walk I became increasingly more and more uncomfortable. You see I hate it when people walk so close behind me that they invade my personal space. So I quickened my pace but so did they. I didn't get angry but I got curious. Finally after a few blocks I casually turned around to see who was dogging my tracks but by then the person was gone. I continued on my journey and I no longer felt the presence until a few blocks later. Feeling like I was loosing my mind I quickly looked behind me and there was no one there. By now I had reached the retail part of town with a constant flow of display windows. As I began to get that feeling once more, this time I turned ever so slowly so that I could catch a reflection of the person all up on my butt. It was my butt. Oh, my, God!!! I couldn't believe it. My butt had gotten sooooooo big that…

Weight will quietly sneak up on you. I gained my weight a little at a time about a pound and a half every month on average, about fifteen pounds a year. I knew I was gaining weight as the years went by because I had to buy and make larger clothing but I still didn't realize how large I had become until I was well over three hundred pounds. I've had a weight problem all my life so I was accustomed to being over weight but not morbidly obese. One of my turning points was when I went to the doctor with stomach pains and he asked me to get up on the examining table. I'm already short so I normally have a hard time getting on the table. But this time as I began to get on the table the back of the table went up like a teeter-totter. Oh the horror! Please, please don't let this become you. Forget about everybody. This is something you have to do for yourself. Now I'm not saying that it doesn't matter what other people think because it does. We still have to live in the world with other people and try to function in society with its ever changing standards of acceptance.

My doctor asked me one day what was my main reason for wanting to lose weight. I knew the answer she wanted to hear but being an honest person I told her the truth.

My health is the number one reason I said but looks are just as important. She frowned and said "I don't think you have your priorities straight". You see I know that my health is the most important reason but lets face it we live in a visual world, a time where an artist's CD doesn't sell unless he/she releases a video first. And never mind how good you can sing if you're fat and unattractive (especially females). Looks are only slightly less important than your health because you have to survive in a visual world. We must live in reality people.

People tell me all the time how attractive I am but I know to attract the typical man, I need to lose weight. Good thing I don't like the typical man, *bwaaaaaaah*!

Men fall in lust with women body parts but a real man falls in love with the whole woman. All of us have heard men say, I'm a breast man, I'm a leg man, or I'm a booty man. And though that may be their preference most men are attracted to a woman's all around appearance. That's why we hear men call women butterheads (Everything looks good but her head). So then why so much fuss over tig-o-bitties? What is the fascination that men have with breast? I mean breast of all sizes. Men just love breast. And does size matter? Hecks yeah! I don't care how pretty your face is, a nice set of tig-o-bitties will distract them every time. Even gay men like tig-o-bitties. Sorry to say for women, especially those with tiny bite-sized breasts, (pun intended) size do matter to most men. Now I know that I'm going to get hate mail from both men and women on this but if you disagree with me, know that you're in the minority. Like I said before size always matters. I don't care what the subject, size always matters. Hand size matters, waist size matters, butt size matters, penis size matters, the size of your lips matters and yes breast size does matter.

To the unbeliever, open your mind to what I'm saying for a moment. Men are aroused by the size of a woman's breasts that's why there're so many tittie bars (excuse the terminology but that's what they call um) and plastic surgeons raking in millions of dollars a year.

When you ask men how they feel about breast size most of the time you will not get a real answer. Men will tell women what they think they want to hear, especially boyfriends and husbands. But if you want the truth, the whole truth, talk to that guy friend you have. You know the one guy friend we all have that's just our homie. He will spill his guts. He'll tell you everything you ever wanted to know about how men feel on a variety of subjects. Now, this cannot be a guy that wishes he were your man. This has to be a good male friend or just any random guy you feel comfortable enough with to talk to. Single men tend to be more forthcoming because giving honest answers carries no repercussions.

So if you don't have Tig-O-Bitties do you buy them? Wellllll? I can't answer that. Anybody who knows me knows that I got a pair that will make a grown man…oops, sorry I digress. If you're considering getting fake breast or implants, ask yourself these questions.

Who am I doing this for?

What is my reason?

If your answer to these two questions is a man, don't do it but if not move on to the next questions.

When can I get time off for the procedure and recovery?

Who will perform the procedure and where (extremely important)?

And last but not least can I afford it?

Again I say men like breast. So that means real or fake. But does it matter if they're real or not and which do they prefer? Ahhhhhhh, the age old question. So I asked.

Men say that they don't care if a woman's breasts are fake when they're watching strippers or porn. We hear women (mostly haters) say, "Those are fake!" And the men respond, "We don't care!" But when it comes to which ones they want to have at home? Ninety percent will tell you real ones. Billy's wife decided to get breast implants. Even though Billy was pleased with the size of his wife's breast Millie just had to have larger breast. While Millie was in surgery Billy went to the hospital's cafeteria for lunch. He ordered the day's special. Tears filled his eyes as the waitress placed his chicken dinner before him. Sir is there something wrong she asked. Billy looked at the waitress and replied, I just realized that this is the only time I'll ever have natural breast in my mouth ever again. *Ahhhhhhhhhhhhh,* that was so funny. You see men are drawn to things that are esthetically pleasing (looks good) but they stay with things that are pleasurably stimulating (feels good). On the real, I mean for real, men do like big breasts but they like small breasts as well. I heard a guy say that he never met a pair that he didn't like.

One thing you should know once a woman has a man hooked, a man who loves her, she doesn't have to worry about her breast size or breast implants. A woman should never get breast implants to please a man. He doesn't care. So in conclusion I guess breast size doesn't always matter… tee hee.

There are some things that you can change and other things you'll have no control over. If you feel your hair's too dark; dye it, too short; get a weave. If you feel your eye's are too dark get color contacts, lashes too short; get false ones. And plastic surgery can just about change every aspect of your face and body. But let's face it there are some things that you just won't be able to change.

I knew a woman who I'll call Queeny (after the queen in snow white.) Queeny was in constant competition with her friend Snowy (tee hee). Queeny was much prettier than her friend and she had a bigger butt which she never mind pointing out. Snowy had bigger breasts which Queeny decided was a bad thing since big breast sag. Everyday in competition each would dress to show off their assets. Snowy would wear tight sweaters and Queeny would wear tight jeans and make fun of flat butt Snowy when she did the same. They would walk down the street and men would holler hey you, the one with the big butt and Queeny knew that they were talking to her. Of course this made Queeny feel great but when Snowy wanted to all she had to do was wear a low cut blouse and shut Queeny down. The men didn't seem to care that Snowy's big breast sagged.

Queeny soon found a way to make her breast appear bigger giving her the edge. The thing is even though Snowy felt the competition I don't think it was as important to her. Some days she'd seem to feed into it and other day she didn't seem to care. When Snowy really wanted to win she would put on a micro mini skirt and show off the longest, prettiest legs you ever wanted to see. Game over! You see you may be pretty but someone else is prettier. Your hair may be long and gorgeous but someone else has longer weave… I mean hair than you. You may have the best p… um, um pie but somebody else's pie may smell better and you know it's more enjoyable to eat pie that smells good…bwaaaaaaah. Okay, I'm sorry I'm just being bad but my point is, to all the young ladies going to extremes to be the baddest "B" out there, just remember there will always be a badder "B" than you (B stands for beauty…of course).

Now, women have it hard from puberty to menopause. With puberty comes menstruation and with menstruation comes discomfort sometimes mild sometimes severe. I had it bad.

Where was Vicodin when I was a teenager? Okay they did have Tylox but I didn't know that until I had oral surgery and we all know that most doctors will let black people suffer before they give them pain meds (I didn't make this up, its been documented by white people… for real). Never the less at seventeen I landed a job working for a doctor. When I started cramping I took everything from Tylenol #2 to Tylenol #4 with a Valium chaser. But even this didn't work. So I suffered. If you have problems like I had seek out a doctor till you get one to listen. No one should have to suffer like I did.

Now with menstruation comes the chance of pregnancy. Yeah, I know you know, so act like you know and stop having unplanned pregnancies. As we get older our chances of getting pregnant becomes slimmer. But as long as you have a period guess what you could still get pregnant. So please remember that until you get to the glorious stage of menopause.

Right, menopause, what a trick! My periods were so bad that all my life I've chanted, "I can't wait till menopause". Hot flashes, so what! No more bleeding. Man, I didn't know what I was talking about.

See before menopause there's perimenopause or pre-menopause. That's when all the fun starts. First there's the little hot flashes and it's funny… at first. Then the night sweats start and that's never funny. You wake up smelling so taint you'll think you fell asleep in the zoo. I did. Then the hot flashes begin to occur more often and become more severe. And as if that wasn't bad enough, then came the oily skin and the acne. You're already aging so now you need acne? What da? Well, the oily skin is the only thing that's greasy because everything else gets dry. Your legs look like crocodile skin and your feet can cut the sheets. You get dry eyes, dry lips, dry hair, dry mouth and dry oops! You know.

But it's menopause it's great right? Sure if you like insomnia or restless sleep. Not to mention weight gain, heart palpations and hair loss. I lost so much hair it looked like I was taking chemotherapy. These things can wreak havoc in your life. But if you keep up with proper nutrition, exercise, take plenty of supplements and use a lot of moisturizer you can get through it. As for the acne humph, I tried all those expensive products and none of them worked for me so I remembered what the teens used when I was younger, Clearasil Vanishing Cream. It helped with the oily skin and cleared the acne up. Thank you Clearasil!

One of my nieces called me one day and the subject of acne came up. She asked me if I thought Proactive worked. I said of course it works because they get people to use it. They have a great marketing strategy, they stress to follow the directions. So, when you go to the trouble to order something from an infomercial and pay a substantial price for it plus shipping and handling guess what, you're going to use it fatefully and as directed but when we buy a less expensive product we tend to not use it fatefully. Most acne meds have the same active ingredient benzoyl peroxide including Proactive. I tried the expensive brand and I did not keep up with the routine (Proactive Solution is a 3-step acne management system) and my skin got worse but when I remembered that the teenagers of my day used Clearasil I was finally able to stop the break outs and start to repair my skin. I love Clearasil Vanishing Cream. Use it as a mask around the house and use less when going out. Sistahs, don't buy the tinted version. Buy the regular version just use a little when going out and rub it in good. Remember beautiful skin is an essential part of a woman's body.

A woman's body just seems to go through a lot of changes that Momma never prepared me for and yes everybody's different. Because everybody's different mothers neglect to give out the information I'm writing about. It's better to know about these things and not need the information than to not have this information and need it.

Our body changes seem to start right around the age of thirty. I discovered my first gray hair right on my thirtieth birthday. It was just standing out like, how U dur'in? That was the beginning of sorrow. Other signs of aging soon followed.

I began to notice that every time I dropped a tear the skin under my eyes would burn. You see as you age the skin under your eyes gets thinner. Not a big thing right? Well as I was examining the skin under my eyes there was something wrong and I just couldn't put my finger on it. It was my eyelashes. Where were they? They were so sparse. Man, everything gets sparse and thin and dry. Why, why, why didn't Mommy tell me this was coming?

Next I noticed that my fingernails that were never thick to begin with were getting thinner. Thank God I had a thick head of hair because it was getting thinner also.

Ladies who are blessed with long luscious thick heads of hair will begin to notice their hair thinning right around the age of thirty. You see y'all all young and pretty and you think these are little things but they will be devastating when they happen because there are so many little things.

Next comes the receding hairline, the receding gums and the ridges on your teeth. Everybody knows about the hairline and we've all noticed the way older folk's teeth look but you just can't imagine how it is to have receding gums. Your gums seem to become pushed back and loose around your teeth and all of a sudden the popcorn that you used to love that use to just get a little stuck in your teeth becomes your worse enemy. As a matter of fact anything with fiber just seems to escape being swallowed, by running under your gums. And don't have a few fillings in your teeth, between the foods that gets under your gums and in your fillings you could store a meal.

One time the gums under my two front teeth got really sore. Every day it got more and more painful and swollen and it felt as though something was stuck up under them. No matter how I brushed and flossed I couldn't seem to find anything under there. Just when I felt I'd go mad, I finally was able to push my gums back a little with my thumb nail and pull down a popcorn husk. When did I have popcorn, I wondered? Oh yeah, three weeks ago. Receding gums hum, yeah.

Feet become another issue. Your feet seem to stay crusty not to mention the liver spots on the bottom of your feet and the palm of your hands. I have to pumice my feet all winter long as where in times past I only had to do it once. Then I would just keep my feet nice and moisturized all winter long. Now my feet have to be moisturized in the summer too.

Thirty can be a trying age. No wonder women stay twenty nine for years. After the age of thirty, women are more prone to things like yeast infections. Even frequent bubble baths are risky. Antibiotics, once your friend is now your enemy. Every time you pick up a bottle of antibiotics you have to pick up something for a yeast infection.

As we continue to age by the grace of God, we worry about the new gray hairs we seem to find daily and we start to wonder, when will the wrinkles come? But modern science is our friend. No longer can you tell the age of a woman by the color of her hair. And anti-wrinkle creams really do work. And that Osteo Bi-Flex is a magic pill to all who have joint issues. I take the advanced triple strength and it works even at my weight.

So as we age we will continue to encounter different little things such as that afro that just appears in each nostril one day out of nowhere. Don't worry this usually doesn't take place till you're well into your sixties. But you know what I never thought about? All the hair on your body eventually turns grey. Yep, there too! Hee, hee, hee, hee! You know I never thought about it but one day my Bad Auntie was talking about it and I was cracking-up.

Chapter 5

A Black Woman's Body

Black women should be aware of some subtle differences in our bodies. Black women have higher rates of many illnesses, such as hypertension, breast cancer, stroke, and lupus. For this reason they really need to take more interest in preventive health care. This is good advice for all women but women of color have a few extra problems especially dark women. For the more serious problems please keep up with your yearly exams and don't put off seeing your doctor when you have symptoms of a potentially serious illness.

Now having said that, the one subject I would like to touch on is the skin problems that darker women face.

Black women especially the darker women are subject to more skin problems than anyone else. Some of the Common skin problems they face are: Hyper-pigmentation, Vitiligo, Pityriasis-alba, Flesh moles, Hypertrophic scars and Keloids.

I used to have the most beautiful skin. I managed to make it through puberty without acne or anything other problem. I've always had compassion for kids with acne and I was so grateful for having escaped that fate, or so I thought. I didn't begin to have trouble with acne until much later in life. It started with one huge pimple that healed and left a huge dark spot behind. After that came another one and another one and another one until my beautiful skin was covered. I tried every acne product

I could get my hands on and even a few homemade remedies but as fast as it would clear up I would break out again. With each breakout I received more black spots until my beautiful flawless skin was peppered with dots. Being a dark complexioned woman made me more prone to spotting. This is called Hyper-pigmentation. Hyper-pigmentation frequently occurs after a skin injury or as a result of acne or eczema. Often, some of these dark spots will fade on their own but sometimes, chemical peels, microdermabrasion or bleaching medication may be your best solution.

Dark women of color just seem to be susceptible to more skin problems than others. There are few conditions that we should be aware of besides Hyper-pigmentation.

Y'all remember that girl y'all used to pick at, you know the one you called cow face because she had huge white patches on her face? Yeah, y'all wrong for that. Vitiligo is a devastating skin disorder in which little by little pigment cells are destroyed and replaced with white patches.. Some cases can be simply treated with cortisone creams, but other treatments can be as drastic as skin grafting.

Pityriasis-alba, not quite as devastating as Vitiligo, causes round, light patches of scaly skin, on the face and upper arms. It is a common skin condition mostly occurring in children. Pityriasis-alba is more often seen in males than females and can be controlled with the use of a good moisturizing cream. This condition may actually occur more in light-skinned children, but is more obvious in those of a darker complexion.

One skin condition that is so common in my family is those blasted Flesh moles. These moles are seen almost exclusively in African Americans or Black people as I prefer to call us. Facial Moles or Dermatosis Papulosa Nigra are non-cancerous flesh moles that often appear on the cheeks. For the most part we just endure them but sometimes they might grow on the neck or too close to the eyes and can become a nuisance. If you find them to be bothersome they can be surgically removed.

Hypertrophic scars and keloids look similar but Hypertrophic scars don't get as big as keloids and with a little luck they may even out or fade with time. Hypertrophic scars are the result of the body overproducing collagen, causing scaring to be raised above the surrounding skin. Keloid scars are much more serious. They can grow indefinitely into large unsightly tumors sometimes disfiguring the body. Both hypertrophic and keloid scars are most common in darker-skinned people but some people are genetically susceptible to these types of scarring. They can be caused by piercing (you remember the girl y'all called bubble ear, yeah, y'all wrong for that), surgery and even acne. Methods of removal are cortisone injections or laser treatments but keloids tend to grow back. After a wound has occurred to the skin both skin cells and tissue cells begin multiplying forming a scar to hold the wound closed. With keloids, the cells continue to multiply even after the wound is closed. Keloids develop above the surface of the skin to form a large mass of scar tissue.

Black women, we must be extra careful in taking care of our skin.

Yes, we do need sunscreen. A lot of black people don't know that we need sunscreen. For some reason some of us confuse it with suntan lotion. Sunscreen protects you from the sun allowing you to age more gracefully. People with dark skin already age a lot slower than others because they have more melanin in their skin and if they use sun block they can age even more beautifully.

Chapter 6

Dress to Impress

I hate when my nieces throw something on just to run to the store. Everybody does it right? Wrong, I don't. I believe we should look good at all times. Did you know it's just as easy to put on a cute outfit as it is to put on a tacky outfit? I heard a young lady say that she just threw on a pair of jeans and an ugly t-shirt to go to the store. I said why. Why do you even own an ugly t-shirt? How many times have you been caught outside the house looking a hot mess? You think that you can just run to the store grab one thing real quick and just run back home. It'll only take about fifteen minutes. In those fifteen minutes you manage to run into your ex-boyfriend or even worse his new girlfriend. There you stand in the checkout line looking pitiful with a stained sweat-suit on and a raggedy ponytail on your head holding a box of Chunky Donkey ice cream. Now you want to scream. So to make yourself feel better you start talking to yourself saying that's okay, everybody knows that I can be fierce when I want to. But deep inside you feel sick because you got caught looking a hot monkey mess.

I think people should look their best at all times especially women. You should always look good and please smell good because you never know who you'll bump into.

I know a lady who was doing some heavy house cleaning and lost track of the time. She needed to catch the store before it closed and she only had a few moments to do so. Needless to say by now she didn't smell too fresh but she had to catch the store right? So she figured if she kept her arms down close to her side no one would smell her after all she wasn't really musty, just a little taint. As she entered the store who did she run smack dead into? You guessed it that fine guy from high school who she'd been secretly in love with for years. And what did he want but a great big hug. So up went my arms…oops I mean her arms and out came the musk. I was sooooooo; I mean she was sooooooo embarrassed.

We never know who we're going to run into. If you're looking bad you will run into that ex-boyfriend or even a handsome stranger.

At my church they have a habit of quoting the scripture that says be ye also ready. That is to say you should be ready for anything at anytime. You just never know who you're going to run into.

Jasmine had decided to go to the Bay Breeze to let off a little steam after a long day. She had a stressful job interview with Donald, the president of a prestigious institution earlier that day and needed to unwind. She put on her favorite "do-me" dress and told her husband that she was going out with the girls. Yeah, she had a husband. While she was standing at the bar waiting to order a drink a man standing close by bumped her. Excuse me he said as he turned to apologize. Yelp, it was Donald and there she stood in all her glory, breast out nothing covered but the nipple. Her dress was so short and tight she looked like a cheap hooker. You see some women mistake scanky for sexy. But Donald could tell the difference and Jasmine (not her real name) didn't get the job. The sad thing is that Jasmine is a brilliant young woman but just a little lax in the morals department.

When it comes to dressing, "do you" but if "you" are dirty, tacky, sloppy or scanky please, do somebody else. I once heard someone say you should dress according to your status and station in life. If you're a professional keep a professional image. Choose attire for which you'll receive positive response from people around you because contrary to what you may believe, what people think of you does matter. Your clothing should always be clean and pressed. Yes, it does matter and that spot is not okay and yes we can see it. Your clothes should fit neatly and lay the same whether standing, walking or sitting. The majority of people don't want to see your pubic hair when you sit down and we also don't want to see the stretch marks on the back of your thighs when you stand up.

If your skirt or dress crawls upwards when you walk it's too little. If your shorts or pants crawl up your thighs and bunch up your puss…oops I mean pubic area they are too small. I know y'all heard it all before but here is one that usually confuses y'all. If your skirt or pants is hanging off your waist and fitting tight on your butt, your pants are not too big they are probably too small. Try a larger size. Believe it or not it's your big butt that has the waist band stretched out.

Again dress according to your station. If you're interested in the hip hop industry don't try to sell yourself in a button down suit. If you want a job at a department store do not go to the interview draped in diamonds and gold. They will not hire you if they think you don't need the job. If you want to be a stripper by all means dresses as scanky as you can. Just remember whatever your station in life neat and clean is still always the way to go.

Accessories and make up is also important. The only people who walk around in heavy make-up in the daytime are tacky women and hookers. So you're either one or the other. Your daytime jewelry should also be tasteful. Go easy on the ghetto earrings at job interviews but on club night go ahead, knock yourself out with your door knocker earrings.

Now, just to be clear, there is no right or wrong here just tactful and tacky. You can do whatever you want but at least you'll know why other people seem to get ahead. And maybe getting ahead is not what you want. People measure success in different ways. I measure it by happiness. To me a successful person is the one who finds happiness. So don't look down your nose at nurse's aids, janitors or Wal-mart workers because some of them are poor but happier than you'll ever be. Well, once again I digress.

Okay, hair is another accessory. Ghetto hair-dos always fascinate me. To me they're neither ugly nor pretty, just fascinating. I don't knock them. They're a work of art. And I am an artist. My god daughter who I esteem as the most amazing beautician in the world (and yes I still call them beauticians) is queen of the ghetto stylists. She can do anything. I mean anything. I love to call her a beautician because when an ugly woman sits down in her chair she will get up beautiful. I've seen this with my own eyes. She can do anything from a simple chignon to an extravagant fantasy style. But like clothes every hairstyle has its place. Please don't apply for a corporate job with curly-Qs in the front, waterfalls in the top, finger waves in the back and corn-rows on the side of your head topped with glitter. This might be sharp for the club but not for a job interview. When you sit down in your hairdresser's chair think about what you have planned for the week. If it's business as usual, get anything you want. It's always good to try new things. But if you have something important planned; get a style that fits your plans. Most importantly don't try new styles when you have an important date such as your prom, wedding or high school reunion. Give new hair-dos a test run before important one time occasions like these.

In these days and times hair is as important and fashionable as our wardrobe. A woman can have short hair just above her ears one day and long hair down to her waist the next. Maybe you were born with black hair; it doesn't matter because we can be blond on Monday, brunette on Tuesday, burgundy on Wednesday red-headed on Thursday, auburn on Friday with streaks on Saturday and back to black on Sunday.

Women especially black women have as many wigs, weaves and hair pieces as we do clothing. It is imperative that you know when and where to wear what. Get it? Got it? Good! Whew!

Chapter 7

Make-up and Perfume

Make-up, make-up, make-up! To wear or not to wear, that is the question. Should women wear make-up? Yes, wear it. Please! If you need it, wear it and trust me, some women really need it. Men say they don't like it but they're not being completely honest. You see all the women branded as the most beautiful women in the world wear make-up and if they stop they will lose their title. I used to be hard on girls about make-up. I said no one really needs it. Wrong. I never had acne as a teen but later on it hit me like a ton of bricks leaving spots and uneven tones all over my face. I now use a bronzer that evens my skin tone and occasionally a little spot cover-up. Aging is something you should do gracefully and sometimes a little make-up can help you do just that. As you get older your skin tone can become dull and pale. Your lips also may become dry and dehydrated. A little lip-gloss solves this problem (okay, a lot of lip gloss). And ladies when it comes to choosing lip-gloss we can take a lesson from the kids. Little girls wear sweet flavored lip-gloss. Why…because it taste good. I wear a beautiful slightly tinted sheer flavored lip-gloss. When men say they don't like make-up that means you wear too much. And if you got on that nasty tasting lipstick that they make for adult women, he just might hate it. So my advice which I give to my nieces, switch to strawberry lip-gloss or the flavor of your choice but make it sweet. I hear you. You're saying, I already know that right? Well, we tend to forget. We grow up and we switch to adult make-up and we forget about the smile we used to leave on our teenage boyfriends face.

Make-up serves many purposes. Young ladies use it to make them look older and older women use it to look younger.

Two of my nieces went to the club one night. Only one was old enough to get in. The oldest niece, well over twenty-one had no ID and no make-up on. The club owner allowed the under age one in. She by the way was totally made-up. The one that was of age got denied. Being very small 4'11" tall and 92lbs she needed a little make-up.

Make-up can also cover up blemishes, scars and a bad night's sleep.

So what about perfume? A many divorces can be traced back to a bad choice of perfume…just kidding, but almost. I love perfume. My father calls perfume "Follow me boy." I always wear perfume and every time I would get ready to leave the house my father would say "I smell that follow me boy." I think women should smell good at all times.

So, how do you pick perfume? Well, it depends on whom you're trying to please. When I was younger I wore the fragrance that I was pleased with. I never cared what other people thought about it. If it smelled good to me it had to smell good to everyone else right? That's what I thought. As years went by I learned better.

Important, men and women have different preferences when it comes to perfume. Most men prefer soft, sweet or even fruity fragrances. Women seem to prefer stronger scents.

A loud scent can turn a man away. Men like to get close, if you're lucky that is and a strong perfume can be choking. It's hard for him to talk or do anything else if he can't breathe.

So let's say all your girls tell you that they love your perfume. I mean you can't pass by a woman without her saying, "Ooh girl you smell good, what are you wearing?" If that same perfume chokes your man, trash it.

I usually can tell which perfume a man will love and I just happen to prefer the softer scent myself.

One day I was shopping for perfume and I came across one at Victoria Secrets. It smelled sooooooo good. Well I had my younger sister with me and I was treating her and my Mom who wasn't with us at the time. I showed her the perfume and asked her if she would like a bottle. She said it smelled okay but she preferred a different one. I ask her if she was sure because the one I was buying smelled sooooooo good. She said that she was sure so I bought her what she wanted. I bought myself the complete set. I wore it almost everyday and it soon became my signature fragrance. My niece came to pick me up for lunch and I was wearing it. She made a comment about the fragrance and I told her that men love this type fragrance. "Really?" she replied. I told her "yeah girl, trust your Auntie. Auntie knows." At the restaurant I received many compliments on my perfume from both men and woman. Still not convinced my niece and baby sister did not buy any of the perfume. Then one night baby sis called me to tell me a funny story. She said she was in the mood for going out and she didn't want to go out with the girls so she decided to go hang out with *Craig and nem.* They were hysterically funny as they complained about the condition of the young ladies in the club.

"Look at um" Dae-Dae said. "Every girl in the club is obese. They ain't even out of their twenties yet and they're obese. Look at Shaniqua with her fat self."

Everybody laughed as Shaniqua walked by. Then Dae-Dae got a whiff of Shaniqua.

"Wow, she smells good!" My sister continued to laugh. About fifteen minutes later Shaniqua passes by again. Now all of the guys were intoxicated not with liquor but with her scent. Shaniqua soon passed by again and Dae-Dae became unhinged. "I'm going home with her tonight. Man she smells good" Dae-Dae repeated. "I got to ask her what she's wearing." He followed her through the club and at the first opportunity he asked her what perfume she was wearing and she told him. So I asked my little sister, what was she wearing? Yeah, you guessed it. It was my favorite Vickie Secrets fragrance. I told her that's the one I wear; you know the one I've been telling y'all men love. I then told my niece the Shaniqua story and she and my little sister both ran out and bought the perfume. *Bwaaaaaaah,* Bad Auntie knows best.

When men want to get close they don't want to have a hard time breathing. And you don't want them coughing, choking and sneezing in your ear or on your neck. So think soft. You're soft. Speak soft and wear a soft fragrance.

If you can't figure out what fragrance is right, try a food scent. These usually work. Sugar Cookie is another one that will have them following you home. So handle with care. You may get more attention than you want.

In closing I got to stay true. Men also like some of what I like to call "stanky scents." Oh boy. Wheeeeeew! Stanky scents are those perfumes out there that kind of smell like well… puss, I mean poontang. Yes, they're out there. Now these fragrances are strong and yet men still seem to favor them. Humm, I wonder why. But these are the strong fragrances that many women do not like.

One lady received this type fragrance as a free gift with purchase. Now I want you to note that this was a very expensive perfume. She decided to wear it one night and she put it on generously. As she walked around the house she kept smelling poontang. It wasn't long before she realized that it was herself that she smelled. She said that she had to wash it all off. The woman tried to give the perfume to her sister. The sister took one whiff and said, "Nooooooo it smells like poontang." Needless to say they broke out laughing.

Later she asked her husband to smell the perfume. Curious she asked, "Do you like it?"

"Yeah," he replied.

"Yuck, it smells like poontang."

"I know" he replied this time with a wide smile on his face. So I guess there's an exception to the strong perfume rule if you don't mind walking around smelling like poontang.

Chapter 8

Let's talk about hair.

If I could have my way my hair would be to my waist. I love long hair. Some women say they don't like long hair but usually that's the bald headed ones who can't grow any or the ones with that "good hair" that can grow all they want.

Long hair to me is the most beautiful and I know I'm not alone in my thinking because the weave stores are making billions. I might have been the one who took them up to one billion served. Gurrrrrrl, I wish I had all the money back that I've spent on weaves; I could get out of debt. But let's face it weave is one of the best things to happen to black women since the invention of the straightening comb. I love it for its versatility. The problem is some people talk about it like it's a sin or a disgrace to the black race. Bull-lony!

I have wash and wear hair and I thank God and my ancestor's white slave owners for it (no letters please). So all I have to do to look decent is add water and a little Murray's and tah-dah. Convenient, yeah but not having long hair I always need to add a hairpiece in order to give myself a style. It's simple but effective.

This is a fast pace world we live in and wigs, weaves and hair pieces have relieved a lot of stress from our lives. You see weaves don't "go back". How many times have you straightened your hair only to have it go back as soon as you got to your event? You leave the house looking hot and come home looking a hot mess.

One of my nieces told me the funniest story. She said that she and a friend had a function to attend and she having long hair decided to wear it down. She looked beautiful as she left the house, she and her friend with their beautiful un-permed, chemical free hair. When they arrived at their destination they soon saw that everyone there had fake hair. Feeling proud and superior they took their seats to enjoy the show. At the end of the nights she and her friend had a nice frizzy head of hair and everyone else look the same way they looked when they had arrived. Needless to say my niece now wears weave to important functions and also when she goes clubbing. Nothing sweats out a hair-do like dancing. Now you can sweat out a weave but it stands a better chance than natural hair. And speaking of natural hair, sometimes natural hair needs a little enhancement.

So, now you're thirty, just thirty and the gray hair seems to come in with a vengeance and every since you could remember you have complimented older women on how beautiful their gray hair was. But now it's on your head and it's not so cute. Do you dye it? Hecks yeah! I have a rule if by the time my hair turns gray, if I haven't lost my weight I will dye my hair. But that's my personal rule. You see I can take being fat or being gray but not being fat and gray. Nooooooooooooooo no!

Some people say that natural hair is healthier but that's not necessarily true. I see women with long beautiful permed hair. They take good care of it. Split and damaged ends should be trimmed. Split ends have nothing to due with hair growth but your hair looks healthier when the damaged ends are removed. Hair grows at a rate of approximately one third to one half inch per month. The exception that proves the rule is people who are just genetically inclined to grow long hair fast or pregnant women.

So what's the secret to achieving long hair? Keep the hair you have from falling out while the new hair grows in. This sounds simple but it's harder to do than it sounds. Do you ever wonder why dreadlocks grow so long? It's because you never comb them so the hair is never being combed off of your head. So you just keep twisting it up as it grows. At a rate of six inches a year that's a lot of hair, the only problem with that is the above mentioned, you can't comb it. So when you're ready for a new style you have to what? That's right cut it off.

Proper nutrition and hair care are essential for growing healthy long hair. Here are a few tips I've gotten over the years from the professionals.

1. Keep your hair clean and conditioned.
2. Take vitamin and mineral supplements.
3. Hair is made up of protein so eat plenty of protein.
4. Try adding flaxseed to your diet.

5. Only use a boar bristle brush
6. Never brush your hair when wet, use a wide tooth comb.
7. Try using natural dyes like henna and indigo.
8. Don't use too small combs or snatch your hair.
9. Black women, keep hair moisturized!!!
10. Sleep in a silk or satin cap or on a silk/satin pillow case.

When it comes to hair care everybody has their own ideals as to what to do and what not to do. Beauticians, hair dressers, cosmetologist, stylist or what ever the heck they're calling themselves today are not always right. Remember black women these people got their schooling from institutions that specialized in the study of Caucasian hair. Caucasian, *bwaaaaaaah,* I like that word Caucasian. I think I'll name my first child Caucasian. Okay, just kidding. But really, if you're taking care of your hair and it's healthy and growing keep doing what you're doing and forget what other people (including myself), tell you, obviously you're doing something right.

There is so much false information circulation around that some times you just don't know what to believe so let's go over a few.

Cutting your hair will not make it grow. It does look healthier because all the split ends are gone making your hair look smoother and thicker. I have noticed although that hair kept trimmed seems to fall out less and of course grow more evenly.

Perms don't take your hair out. If you're wearing a perm you must take care of your perm. If your hair falls out nine times out of ten you did not take proper care of your perm. Now notice I said nine times out of ten. Not everybody can wear a perm.

As with perms the same thing can be said of dyes. Dying your hair will not cause it to fall out if you take the necessary precautions. If your hair is falling out you're either allergic or you're doing something wrong. I know people who have worn their hair permed and dyed from puberty thru menopause and to the casket. We bury them at ninety years old with a full head of beautiful luster silky, dark and lovely hair… tee-hee.

Now some of the things you hear are true and the one that tripped me out was the one about smoking. Smoking can cause your hair to turn gray. Wow, good thing I never smoked.

Chapter 9

Dating

Dating is every girl's favorite subject. My nieces of all ages have always talked to me especially about their man problems. My mother would always have to pry a conversation out of her grandchildren as where I had the opposite problem. One day she asked me, how do you get them to talk? I told her just talk about boys. No matter the age, girls like to talk about boys. They may go from icky to yummy and even back to icky but girls like to talk about boys.

So what should we be looking for in a guy? First of all he should have a great personality and a good sense of humor. And the bible says not to be "unequally yoked" with unbelievers (II Corinthians 6:14) right? *Bwaaaaaaah!* That's a mother's answer. We can marry a saved believer and still not be "equally yoked." It has been said that too many women marry because of animal attraction or physical needs and that this will lead to a failed marriage. But a good personality alone does not a good relationship make.

Let's face it relationships are physical as much as they are spiritual and/or emotional. When we get married it's because of our bodies. You don't need to get married to join together two good personalities. So since it's his body you're marring, there better be something about his body you like. Therefore I say LOOKS COME FIRST, personality second. If he doesn't look good "he can't get none." Yeah I said it! Looks come first.

Warning! There is one thing that trumps looks and that is what I call "the cool factor." Oh my God! A cool dude and/or a guy that can keep you laughing will catch you off guard! The next thing you know you'll be talking bout, "He so fine." He might look like a rat eating corn but he's so cool he has you mesmerized.

Every since my nieces started talking to me about men I've warned them, stay away from cool ugly dudes because one day you'll find yourself waking up next to one. They can be irresistible.

Now honestly the type of man you get with is a matter of personal preference and there are several types of men. There are Rich men, Poor men, Young men, Old men, Fine men, Ugly men, the Church brothers and that yum…yum Thug from the street just to name a few. I have found a use for every type except the Ugly man. I'm sorry but no matter how hard I try, I just can't find use for an Ugly man. I've heard some women say they love ugly men. Well I say help yourself you won't get any trouble out of me. But what ever your personality, get the one that's right for you. That "evenly yoked together" saying is true. So if you're a "gold digger" you will never be happy with the poor man. And if you love to party the church brother might not be your best choice. You see opposites may attract but that doesn't mean they make each other happy. Usually this couple will end up in misery that is until the divorce.

So let's talk about these men starting with *Rich men.* I started with them because um… um… um…sorry, I don't know a "D" thing about them *(Oh, "D" stands for dumb because y'all know I don't cuss).* So if anybody knows anything about rich men call me. My phone number is 814-504-????. *Ahhhhhhhhh! Tee-hee!*

So, on to the *Poor-man* now this is something I know a little about. Ain't *nut'in* wrong with a poor man. You know what they say, *"He gat dat ambition."*

Quality poor men are creative. They write you poetry when they can't buy you a present. They can make the most romantic evening out of nothing. They will do without just to buy you something and they will go to any lengths to take care of their family.

I once knew a poor man whose landlord didn't pay their water bill. The city water department came and turned their water off. This man collected trashcans filled with water daily for a family of five. That means drinking water, water to bathe with and water to flush the toilet. Now if that wasn't enough, the toilet clogged up. Do you know what this man did? Every time his wife and kids used the toilet he would scoop out the mess, dig a whole and burry it in the ground. Yes he did! What other man would have known what to do with that "S" *("S" stands for stuff because y'all know I don't cuss)*? So there is something to be said about poor men, if nothing else they are resilient. Never the less, they're not my choice. No woman sets out to find a poor man but he's not hard to love. Now let's move on to the Young-man.

Young-men are strong, active, attentive, and attractive, out going, energetic, full of life, stupid, juvenile, cunning, humorous and youthfully handsome. Notice how I hid broke, stupid and juvenile between the good stuff. Oops, I didn't mention broke? Yeah, a lot of times they tend to be a little financially challenged.

I have a confession to make. I got a thing for young men. When I was young I liked older boys, as I got older I preferred men my age but now hummmmm, those young dudes "*bout-sta*" turn me out. *Bwaaaaaaah!* Okay, okay, okay for real they are tempting.

Oooooooooh! I love me a young man! But *gurrrl* a young man will "tap dat um…tail." Yeah, that tail. I *betcha* Momma didn't tell you that. They just seem to have a shorter fuse than the others. So if you get with a younger man, (meaning you're significantly older than he is) please don't get smart with him, you'll frustrate him and he will beat you. They haven't evolved enough yet as to where they can handle our smart mouths. And let's face it sisters, most of us have smart mouths. It ain't just me.

Younger men have to be handled. Yep, I said it. I know handling people is supposed to be a bad thing but it's a necessary thing that is if you want peace, which brings me to them being stupid. Their stupidity makes them easy to handle but you will find yourself giving up a lot of who you are in order to please him and you may also have to support him. In return you will probably get a man who is lively, loves to take you out, keeps you laughing hysterically I might add and I will not even get into the obvious physical attributes. It's really not that kind of book. But "y'all know." *Bwaaaaaaah!*

*Note; when young men get close to thirty, be careful because that's when they begin to learn how to read us. They may indeed be younger than you but they're not so young anymore. Don't play them for stupid, you might get embarrassed. I found this out the hard way.

Older men are of course different from the young man. They tend to be more settled and more able to deal with our mouths than the young man. Older men are generally not as active, more apt to stay at home and can ignore you for days. I know a lot of women who only date old men…but then again I know a lot of women who only date married men. Okay, I digress.

Where younger men may be dense older men are wiser, where the younger man is juvenile older men are more mature. What older men lose in attentiveness, they make up in compassion. And what they lose in vitality, they more than make up in skills. Ok, I'm being nice but… *ain't nuth'in* wrong with an old man and if he's lived right he's probably got "a little *sump'in sump'in*" saved up. So if you're planning to get with an older man, (meaning he's significantly older than you) know what you're getting into. He can be condescending. He'll love your adult attributes but he'll still treat you like a child. No matter how sweet he is he can't help it. Older men must be in control. Do not challenge their authority or like the young man he... will... beat... you.

Single *Churchmen!* Ok...where are they? They sure aren't at church. For real!!! I checked!!!

There are so few men getting saved that I almost skipped over them but that wouldn't be right. Besides, every girl needs to know what she's in for if she marries a churchman.

Now when I say churchman I mean saved for real. Not those pretenders. I'm talking about the guys that are truly walking with God, no clubbing, smoking, drinking or cussing just good clean living. I'm not talking about the ones whose sentences always starts with "ain't nothing wrong with... or it's alright to...and my personal favorite; don't worry baby, it only seems nasty the first time"

Mommies will tell you that you need a good churchman and she's right. I can't argue with that but... I'm an Auntie so I got to keep it factual. Churchmen come with mess too. The good thing about them is they're legit. You don't find yourself bailing them out of jail every time you look around. They don't cheat on you. They don't gamble your money away and my favorite, they come home at night, obvious right? So let's get to the bad. They're sometimes sexist, chauvinistic, domineering, demanding, and they can also be quite boring at times. But do you know what really sets me off? Before some of these men got in the church "they ugly selves" couldn't buy a woman. But now they're in the church where the women out number them twenty to one and they have the nerve to get cocky. They walk around like they're literally God's gift to women. It's enough to make me hurl.

If you can find a chivalrous churchman that's great but a lot of them mistake chivalry with chauvinist. But he is a churchman and a good churchman can be reasoned with. I'm basically a traditional woman because I find that traditional ideals are based in reality. I love the traditional man that walks me home in the dark or moves to the side by the curb, because he wants to protect me from the streets. Now to my liberated women, I know you can protect yourselves but don't be mad at me. I'm ecstatic when a man pays for my meals, carries my bags or offers me his coat when I'm cold. And again to my liberated sisters, don't be mad at me 'cause I will cook my man a home cooked meal, rub his aching back and wash his dirty drawers. I may not wait on him hand and foot all the time but I'm certainly not above it. I will watch the games with him when he wants me to and I know how to get my stroll on when he wants to be with his boys. I must have a churchman but he has got to be "fine" (and just a little thuggish). *Oops!* I'm sorry. But speaking of the thuggish man, *they're so much fun you gotta get you one*. Kidding, kidding.

There are different types of *Thugs*. Some thugs are just "urban" type men, you know, with that swagger. Ummmmm… that swagger! They're usually raised in the ghetto, the inner city or low-income area of town. But then there're the other ones. The ones that sell drugs, stolen goods, bootleg DVDs, mix-tapes or sneakers out the trunk of their car. I think there're all sexy but that's just me. When I'm with them I always feel safe when in reality sometimes I should feel the opposite way. Oh help me but God I love them. They give me the swirlies in the pit of my stomach. There's something about that street swagger and I can tell if it's real. Either you have it or you don't. It's something that you just can't fake. Man, if I could find a thug that'll go to church but keep that swagger, work a real job but still know how to hustle…it's on! But I'm going to try to be realistic here. A thug is not really the best choice for a lifetime mate. A "good girl" won't be able to deal with his lifestyle for too long. He hustles all night and sleeps all day. He's balling one minute and broke the next. He's volatile, unpredictable, unstable, hot-blooded and short tempered. Some really know how to get that money and although you may love all the diamonds and gold jewelry he buys for you, you'll end up pawning them to get his "A" out of jail (A stands for appendages because y'all know I don't cuss).

I know women who were living large, had a nice project laid out in Rent-a-Center furniture, a nice car on spinners that their man paid cash for (can't leave a paper trail) the latest gear, their nails done or as they say where I'm from "their nails did" and a new hair-do every week. But after their men went to jail they spent the next five to ten years *"putting something on his books."*

Do you know what's scary? Thugs appeal to women from every socioeconomic background. That's just how it is and always will be. No I don't recommend them, not for my nieces but there is someone for everyone. So if you're a hoe or a street girl, you might want to get with a thug. That's entirely up to you. Maybe you're not a hoe but have those *"hoe-ish"* tendencies. Or maybe you are just a compassionate woman with longsuffering and able to abide his foolish ways until he changes. If you can out last his foolish ways until he changes you'll most likely end up with the best man of the bunch. Because when they change, they change. And all the energy they used to give to the streets they now give to you.

It has been my observation that when Thugs settle down they make the best mates. Those who used to run around and never seem to come home now can't get enough of being around you. They become the most faithful men and they seem to more than love and adore their wives. Too bad they don't come with a guarantee or I'd surly get me one, (*I just might anyway, tee-hee*). God bless you, the women who can hold out!

So let's talk about *Fine men vs. Ugly men.* Fine men are e*rrrrrrrr um*.............well, fine. What? Okay, okay, they are easy on the eye. I mean it's a no-brainer. He's a turn-on. But some can be vain, conceded (not the same thing), arrogant and unfaithful. It's not that there're bigger cheaters by nature it's just they have more opportunities. If you're a jealous type woman you might not want to get with that *"super"* fine man. Women throw themselves at fine men incessantly. And I'm sorry but unless he's saved and sanctified, he going to catch one sooner or later. So just be ready to forgive him, that is, if you really want him.

Many women have a misconception that an ugly man is safer than a fine man but this is not true. They say they like ugly men because they don't cheat. Wrong! Listen good, ladies, UGLY MEN DON'T KNOW THERE'RE UGLY and the ones who do, say to themselves, "I must not be ugly, after all I pulled her". They then develop an ego out of this world. When a "pretty woman gets with an ugly man she validates him. She makes him attractive to other women who in the past would have never given him the time of day. He then gains more and more confidence and even begins to get a little swagg. So they do everything a Fine man does. Therefore if you choose to get with an Ugly man, get with him because you love him.

Some folks get angry with me because I say that I don't like ugly men but remember beauty is in the eye of the beholder and the finest man in the world to me might be ugly to you. So relax people ugly is just an opinion.

SEX

Sex, this is another subject I know nothing about. So what do I tell my unwed nieces? Don't Do It!!! Bwaaaaaaah! Now, having said that, I want you to know that I'm not stupid. Aunties of the world must be prepared. Your nieces might ask you about anything. Why, because "Auntie knows". A long debated question has been should you teach your child about birth control. Thank God I'm not a mother because I don't have a dilemma. I tell them everything they want to know. I know that unless there're saved in church, the majority of adolescents engage in premarital sex, so I say be as safe as possible. I might get in trouble with the church for saying this but I love the fact that there are such things as condoms. Do I preach abstinence? Yes, yes, yes. But I want my nieces and nephews to know all about condoms. I know that teenage pregnancy is a huge problem but my major concern is sexually transmitted diseases. An unplanned pregnancy can be classified as an "oops!" Then life goes on. But HIV and AIDS are not "oops!" and life doesn't just go on. As a matter of fact death is the usual outcome. Every time I find out that one of my unwed nieces or nephews are expecting I just want to hit them over the head with a brick wrapped in an HIV pamphlet. They think that I'm angry because of the unplanned pregnancy and because there're not married. That's not it. I don't like it but what angers me the most is the carelessness. To the nieces of the world, when you chose not to use a condom, instead of giving you a baby that man could have given you AIDS. And to the nephews of the world, when you chose not to use a condom, instead of getting a baby from that woman you could have gotten AIDS. How many billions of dollars of the tax payers money does the government have to use to keep repeating one little sentence? Huh? What is your damage!!! I mean what the frail!!! Use a frickin condom!!! AIDS is real. Your cousin got it and you don't even know it.

Condoms aren't scary. They're user friendly. They come in all different colors, textures, shapes and sizes and they even come in flavors (because some of y'all nasty).

Condoms are made in different lengths and widths, kind of like pantyhose, get the right size.

Condoms are not indestructible. They are usually made of latex or polyurethane and you should know the difference between the two. Proper use of a condom is essential or you may as well not use one at all. Latex condoms can disintegrate if you use them with the wrong lubricant. Latex condoms can only be used with water based lubricants. So please people no Vaseline. Tee hee. Petroleum jelly or any other oil based lubricant will break down the latex. Some people have an allergic reaction to latex and should use polyurethane condoms instead.

Polyurethane condoms are made of plastic. They say more lubrication is needed and you can use both oil and water based lubricants with them.

So which is better? I don't know. One should be as good as the other the choice is yours. More importantly one should be just as strong as the other and the chance of them breaking is very small if you use them correctly. Also please remember, condoms do have an expiration date. And if it feels sticky or brittle it's no good. Throw it away and replace it with a new one.

They say that sexually active teens are more likely to be depressed and to attempt suicide than virgins. Well I don't know who did the research but not being sexually active made me want to kill myself, *bwaaaaaaah*. They also say that more than 65% of sexually active teens wish they had waited but that's kind of like you wishing you hadn't eaten that last piece of cake. But it was so good going in...the cake that is. Some people try to scare adolescences into celibacy by telling them terrifying facts and statistics but this will never work because raging hormones are stronger than words. Let's face it when you reach a certain age sexual desire at times can be somewhat overwhelming. When we're hungry we eat, when we're thirsty we drink and when we're sexually aroused we naturally want to have sex. And if you think you're in love...well.

Before they lay down most kids know that they could get infected with a sexually transmitted infection (STI) like AIDS,

Herpes, Syphilis, Gonorrhea or Chlamydia, a major cause of infertility. And thanks to all the PSAs we know that about 50% of sexually active adolescents are infected with the Human Papilloma Virus (HPV) which causes 99% of cervical cancer.

The National Institutes of Health report that condoms are not 100% effective in reducing STI risk. Condoms, if used 100% of the time, reduce the risk of HIV by 85%; but I was surprised to learn that they only reduce the infection rate of Chlamydia and Gonorrhea by 50% and condoms do not reduce the infection risk for HPV at all. Also, let's not forget about Genital Herpes *"the gift that keeps on giving"* condoms also only reduce the infection rate of this disease by 50%. So on to that dreaded subject, Abstinence.

Sexual abstinence is a decision to abstain from sexual activity. The decision is usually based on moral or religious beliefs and sometimes because of health issues. Most people have a different idea of the meaning of sexual abstinence. The most common meaning of sexual abstinence is not having sexual intercourse. Some feel that it's okay to hold hands, cuddle, hug and kiss but others feel it to be unacceptable behavior. Your view as to what is acceptable may depend upon your purpose for abstinence.

Saved religious people do not participate in premarital sex therefore with them abstinence is a way of life before marriage. This is also true but rare with people of high moral standards. Unfortunately our society is in a state of moral decay. A virgin used to be looked upon as a jewel, someone to be proud of. Now the poor girl in school who hasn't "done it" yet is ridiculed and made to feel ashamed. The once popular saying "Why buy the cow when you can get the milk for free" has been replaced with" "You don't buy a car before you test drive it first."

Abstaining from premarital sex is the right way but with today's social standards and all the media influences it will be hard to convince people that premarital sex is wrong. Honestly in a normal adult, male or female the urge to copulate is one of the strongest urges there is. Like I said before when we're hungry we eat, when we're thirsty we drink and when we're sexually aroused we naturally want to have sex.

So now you're married and hopefully in a monogamous relationship. You're not quite ready for children so you're on the pill. Everything is going great. You and your hubby are happy in your little one bedroom apartment. You're twenty and he's twenty-one and you both only have one year of college left. You have a ten year plan which does not include a baby until the fifth year. Then bam! You're pregnant but how? You know you never skipped a pill, so what happened? How did you get pregnant when you were so careful? Well I'll tell you. Remember when you were sick with the flu? You were miserable and you didn't want your hubby to touch you. You went to the doctor and got a prescription for a seven day supply of antibiotics. The doctor said for you to take them all even if you start to feel better, finish the whole prescription. By the third of forth day you're feeling better and decide to give your patiently suffering husband a little sweet loving. And that's how you got pregnant. You see antibiotics can render birth control pills ineffective. A lot of women don't know this and a lot of doctors tend to forget to tell them this. So ladies it would be a good idea to refrain from sexual activity until you're finished with the antibiotic or use a condom.

Okay, y'all get it? Please practice safe sex and maybe our government won't have to keep spending billions of dollars saying the same thing over and over, use a condom.

***

Now back to dating. We can't talk about dating without talking about cheating. Men do it and so do women; the only major difference is the reason (see chapter 13).

It seems to me that men usually cheat because they got caught-up in some hoe's web. But usually when a woman cheats she went out looking for it. She wanted revenge because he cheated on her or she felt neglected or she got just plain bored with her man.

So now you've cheated on your man but you've come to your senses and you're not going to do it again. You've realized that this is your future husband. Do you tell him? It was just a one night stand. You feel so guilty. Do you tell him? Do you tell him? DO…YOU…TELL…HIM…………………? No! I said

NO! If he doesn't know, leave it alone. It never helps and he'll never forget and your relationship is damaged forever. Don't destroy your relationship cause of a one night stand. So you feel guilty, live with it. It's your own fault and it's better you live with the pain of guilt than to pass the pain over to your innocent man. And if the other man threatens to tell…deny till you die. Don't admit to nothing that can't be proven. You should go into such a complete state of denial that you even convince yourself.

All right, you've been dating a while and you need a commitment but he doesn't. You're dating only him but he doesn't want a real commitment. He says that you're free to date other people because he's so confident that you won't. He never dates other women so what's wrong? Why won't he commit? One might say that he's keeping his options open but the biggest reason is just plain fear. Men are scared of the "lockdown".

So what do you do? Well, you can stay the course and hope one day he'll come around or you could do the unthinkable. Take him up on that "free to date other people" thing. Now this is not without its risks. He may never speak to you again in which case I say good riddance. If you just can't stand the idea of not having him in your life then you must accept your stagnate existence and stay the course.

When asked what made them commit to their relationship most men said that they were in fear of loosing their woman and realized on their own that they didn't want to live without her. This leads me to the other things you might try and they are: playing hard to get or the good old "give him an ultimatum" routine.

Playing hard to get can be tricky. One of my friends told me that I needed to play hard to get with this guy that I was interested in and I disagreed with her. You see I wasn't sure if the guy was interested in me or not. Playing hard to get is a good idea only if you're sure that the man is interested in you otherwise you'll be playing by yourself and I don't like to play with myself…um… I mean by myself.

If you really don't know if the man is interested in you maybe you need to try the seduction game first. It could be really embarrassing if you're playing hard to get and you find out that he doesn't care. So make sure he's interested.

Once you know that a man is interested but he's a little hesitant about getting into a relationship then playing hard to get could be a good strategy. Men really do love the thrill of a chase as long as you don't run too fast. Humans seem to value things more when they have to work for it.

When playing, you have to know when to run, when to walk, when to slow down and when to get caught.

You see playing hard to get can be a dangerous game. It's kind of like Russian roulette. You're taking a big chance and you got to know when to stop.

He's called you nine times and you didn't answer because your plan is to answer the tenth phone call but he got tired at nine and presumed that you just weren't interested in him. So now he's moved on.

He's asked you out three times, you have an excuse every time but you're going to say yes next time. Well next time never comes. You've pulled that trigger one time too many. Boom! You're dead.

Playing hard to get can make you seem more desirable to a lot of guys and some times it is all you need to get a commitment but when all else fails desperate women turn to "The Ultimatum".

"The Ultimatum", does it work? Yep, it works almost ninety percent of the time. Repercussion, these men will cheat on you almost ninety percent of the time. Why, because he was not ready to commit but he didn't want to loose you and he's resentful because of the ultimatum.

When men are afraid of loosing their woman they instinctively make a commitment and tie her down but when given an ultimatum they seem to feel resentful and unsure of their true feelings. Any relationship built on an ultimatum will at best be shaky in the beginning. But sometimes things will work their way out.

Ladies keep in mind that men and women are opposite sex. So tic for tac doesn't work on them. When men cheat and get caught they feel like you are suppose to forgive them because after all they're "just being a man" right? Now ladies the decision is yours. But when you try to get even by cheating on him he just says you're a whore. I don't care how you say "you did it to me", he doesn't think it's the same thing and nothing you can say will convince him otherwise. Now to be honest it is easy to get revenge on a man because lets face it women we are crafty but tic for tac never works. You can't get even by doing the same thing to him that he did to you. Why, because he doesn't get it. He usually feels justified when he did what he did. Anger tends to cloud all reasoning so no matter how you explain that he did the same thing to you and you forgave him; he'll never see it, never, never, never.

Can you change a man? I've heard women give this bad advice for decades. They tell innocent naïve girls that you can train or change a man. This is so not true. I got an email one day that said "Don't imagine you can change a man - unless he's in diapers". And as far as training him, what is he, a puppy? Now this old adage is closer to the truth, "You can't teach an old dog, new tricks".

Men don't change; they fake it until they make it. If you don't like who he is already, leave him alone. Some woman will be glad to love him just the way he is.

Just for Fun

Okay, this is so unrealistic but it's fun!

Exercise: Build the perfect man

Example

1. **He stands………………………..Six feet tall**
2. **He has a body like…………...Terrell Owens** (Dallas Cowboy)
3. **He has eyes like……………...Michael Ealy** (Actor in Barbershop)
4. **He has hair like……………...Snoop**
5. **He has the complexion of…...Clyde R. Jones** (The soul glo man)
6. **He has lips like……………….Mystikal**
7. **He smiles like…………………Shaq**
8. **He walks like………………….Will Smith**
9. **He talks like………………..…T.C. Carson** (Kyle on Living Single)
10. **He smells like Hugo Boss and taste like…oops**

I'm sorry I got carried away, tee-hee.

I can't leave out one of the main ingredients, Habitt's swagg (Oakland rapper/comedian Mark Curry's nephew). **The boi got swagg! So put it all together and add Habitt's swagg and you got my man!**

Now it's your turn to fill in the blanks.

1. **He stands________________________________**
2. **He has a body like___________________________**
3. **He has eyes like______________________________**
4. **He has hair like______________________________**
5. **He has the complexion of_____________________**
6. **He has lips like_______________________________**
7. **He smiles like_______________________________**
8. **He walks like________________________________**
9. **He talks like_________________________________**
10. **He smells like______________________________**

Chapter 10

Understanding Black Men

I love men! I'm supposed to. I am woman! I don't discriminate, not with race that is. He can be black, brown, yellow, red, white or blue. I mean it because I love that blue alien on Star Trek Enterprise. You know the one that called the white people pink skin? I like pink skin too. I don't care as long as he's attractive. Now I still have a preference and that is a tall dark chocolate man. Yes. Now that's just my preference.

I have dated men of many different nationalities but I always come back to my black men. They have got to be the most unique creatures on the face of the earth. I love them. They keep things interesting. They can be totally unpredictable on one hand and completely predictable on the other. This chapter is not just for the sistahs but also for my white sisters that fancy the brothers. Understanding them is paramount so let's talk about some of their likes and dislikes.

Most black men don't like skinny women. I said most. This is not to say that they like fat women but they do like them soft. So, do they like big booties or is this a myth? Not a myth! This is pretty much common knowledge but I felt it was worth verifying.

I believe black men are the easiest to please if you understand them and are willing to do what's necessary. Hummmmm, willing to do what's necessary is the key. The problem is that a lot of sistahs aren't willing to do what's necessary when the thing that's necessary is bull. I know this is a touchy subject but let's tell the truth sistahs, our white counterparts seem to have a better handle on this. Anyway, black men as a whole like to keep it simple. My sister Lisa came up with this formula that may help you. *Feed them, relieve them and hand them the remote.*

I've heard black men say over and over, "Girly needs to learn how to cook." They just seem to love a good home cooked meal and I for one don't mind giving it to them. Good food makes them happy and who wouldn't want to keep their man happy.

Now, I hear what you're saying, you go to work just like him why can't he cook. Well, this is a reality in a lot of relationships. There's no right or wrong here. Every couple should do what's right for them. Now days, couples try to share the work load at home but a woman should know how to cook. If you don't agree with me, that's okay but don't be mad when you find out that your man is cheating on you with the woman you call Fatso Fanny. You know how she got him? He tasted her food. Then every time he came home to no food he'd go to Fanny's for a little snack, then a meal, then…well you know.

Don't misunderstand me. I'm not saying a woman's place is in the kitchen, but you should at lease know your way around one.

So he's all fed. Now he just needs some TV time. Not all of them but you know the type. Give him his remote and leave him alone. Take advantage of this time you get to yourself. You can even go to your room and call your girlfriends and vent about how he pisses you off. What…you know we all do it and so do they. Sometimes he wants you to just sit in the room with him and say nothing. This can be painful but indulge him once in a while. Not all the time but some of the time. If you do it to much you'll get stuck doing it all the time. But do indulge him from time to time.

If you noticed I left out how to relieve him. If I have to tell you, you don't need a man.

Moving right along, did you know that black men seem to hate drama more than any other race? They can't stand for you to show out on them in public. They try to walk away from you slowly as if a knife is stuck in their back. This is when we really show out. We know that they're embarrassed and they just want to get away. And because we know they're embarrassed we pour it on. Oooooooh y'all wrong for that, hee-hee. Okay, so I've done it a time or two. I was wrong. I didn't know any better. I was young. It's so tempting, especially when you know they're embarrassed.

There are some things you just don't do especially to a black man in particularly. Ladies, don't kick them in the stones. I always see women on TV kicking men in their privates and watch the men fall to their knees. But on the streets I see women kick black men in their private, watch him bend down and come up with an upper-cut. See this only makes him angry that you tried to injure something that gives him such pleasure. Now he might have to go home and ice it but the immediate anger that arises in him seems to temporally numb the pain. He gets the strength from somewhere to knock…you…out.

Women can not beat men and if you can well then you're just the exception that proves the rule. In this day and time when men don't mind hitting a woman, we as women need to watch our step (see chapter 11). Do you know how I fight a black man…I call 9-1-1. And I do that from the neighbors' house. You see I'm "kinda" cute and I want to stay that way. There are women who can hit as hard as a man and even match him skill for skill but you'll never be able to take a punch like him. So you loose.

When a woman fights a man and she thinks that she's won, all she has to do is go home and look in the mirror see her ugly scarred up face and realize that she really lost.

I knew two beautiful women who fought all the time. They were known for winning fights but I think of them as the biggest losers because as they got older their face became more and more scarred. By age thirty five one of the ladies looked as if she had been beaten with a bag of nickels every day of her life (okay, so I exaggerated a little) but for the next thirty years all that people could say about her is, she used to be so pretty. The men she fought and beat still look the same so that makes me wonder, who's the real loser.

We have entered a new millennia and the human race has evolved, some things for the better and some for the worse. Most women work out side the home and most men believe that they're supposed to work. I still believe that a man should take care of his woman and family. Now I know that because of the cost of living most women work however my mother never had to. But in all fairness she did marry a real man, a black man, king of the castle.

Yep, black men are still KING OF THE CASTLE. Most white men that I know seem to have a more relaxed attitude with that "King of the Castle Syndrome" but black men seem to be holding steady. They rule the house, make the decisions and what they say goes, right or wrong. They may not tell you what to wear but they'll tell you what "you <u>bet</u> not wear", *bwaaaaaaah!* They are funny. But like I said they can be totally unpredictable on one hand yet completely predictable on the other and when you know your man he's not hard to read. Then life becomes easier.

We women know you can get most men to do anything as long as he thinks it's his idea, especially black men, because the king ain't doing anything unless it's his idea.

I use to teach preschool. One day a few of the mothers, all white, who had become good friends arrived at the school simultaneously to pick up their children. I listened as they discussed a trip they had planned, a little weekend getaway, ladies only. They even invited me. One of the ladies said that she still had to clear it with her husband. The conversation then became more and more animated as each woman began to tell her what she needed to tell her husband and what they had told their husband,

"…and I said this and I said that, and he better this and he better that, and just tell him when and just tell him what."

As they continued to tell the woman how to handle her husband I caught a glimpse of a mother who had quietly come in the room and was also observing the conversation. She never spoke a word but instead looked me straight in the eyes and raised her eyebrows. At first I was puzzled then I realized that she was married to a black man and I couldn't hold my laughter. She smiled and shook her head as if to say …exactly.

All black men really want is respect and as long as they're doing their job and taking care of me I don't mind giving it to them. Be my King!

Now I've heard sooooooo much criticism about black men and I've criticized them myself. It's just that some times I get tired of the endless belly aching about the man keeping them down. A lot of our young men turn to doing illegal things to make a living instead of getting a job and working their way up. To make things worse Sistahs condone it because well, you know we got our man's back. The problem comes when our men go to jail and they always get caught, sooner or later. We need a generation of young black men to realize that they are going to have to suffer a while longer and join the legal world. They have to continue to work twice as hard as everyone else just to get their due until maybe the world someday evolve into a real impartial civilization.

They say black men are like crabs. I thought this was such an intelligent analogy when I first heard it. Now I've learned to hate the whole quote. You see you can put crabs in a jar with no lid and none will get out, at lease that's what they tell me. I've never seen it for sure. But let's suppose it's true. They say that black men can't get anywhere because they will not work together. When they see one trying to get ahead they'll do anything to pull him back down. They also say that black men need to pull together and help one another like the other minority races. Sure, this is true but it's harder for him to do. You see black people are the only minority that didn't come to America voluntarily like the other minorities (who by the way could mostly pass for white).

Our men descend from a long history of men who stood by powerlessly while their wives and daughters were abused and raped, taken from them and sold like cattle. Yeah, I hear you. You say what about the black women. The difference is that our women suffered the pain but our men suffered the pain and the shame of not being able to protect his family. Shamed and degraded, after slavery when black men were able to care for their household and family, that's what they did. Scarred by generations of helplessness, now free, black men tended to their families and that was all. All he cared for was home, period. He measured his own success by how well he took care of his family. So yes it's going to take a lot of time to undo a mind set that has been passed down through generations. I'm not making excuses but… It's easy to criticize, isn't it?

One thing that drives me crazy is the fact that a lot of black men will not talk things over with their wives. So they make needless costly mistakes that could have been avoided if they had only consulted with their mate. But again that pride, that "King of the Castle Syndrome" just gets in the way. I have seen a bunch of black men get together and make the most stupid mistakes why, because they would not let their women have a say so. To them this would be weakness but in actually it would really be strength. Their women had better keep their mouths shut because their only recourse is to hit. Since they'll never be smart enough to battle our wit all they can think of to do is beat us. So we suffer most of the time in silence, take a few hits every now and then and take solace in getting together and talking about them like a dog. But the sad thing about it is, once again everybody loses because King would rather talk things over with his brothers, his sons or his boys rather than his wife like God intended him to. God gave man a woman to be his help but a lot of black men ignore this. It's almost like they think God didn't know what he was doing. They seem to think that the woman was made so that he could have someone to boss around and have sex with. Oh how I wish our black men would wake up. Well, maybe next generation,

Black men are unique, peerless, unrivaled, in a class of their own ah but alas, there are some things you just don't want him to do and that is "fix it". You say fix what? Anything! Girl, call Bob (the white man) *bwaaaaaaah.* I'm telling you white men got boxes full of tools. My big sister had me crying laughing one day. She said when you call a black handyman to fix something he's going to be all day. He'll do a little work, and then he'll realize that he left the tool he needs to finish the job at home. But he'll be right back, hee-hee. After several trips home and back and a couple more to the store he'll finally be finished and then comes the clean-up which you'll have to do. This by the way is usually a bigger mess than it had to be. Now call that white handyman. He comes in with a tool box the size of a mini bar and gets busy. He's usually in and out with minimal mess.

I'm sorry brothers, but I still LOVE y'all.

Chapter 11

He Will Slap You Down

People say that there's no reason for a man to beat a woman with the exception of self-defense. This may be true but there are some things you can do or say to a man that will make him slap you down.

We, women have a habit of talking and talking and talking until we make a man snap. You're not satisfied unless you can get a rise out of him. Then we say, "no one has the rights to tell me to shut-up." Again this is true but some of you will not be quiet until the man knocks you out. Then you're as quiet as a church mouse. That is until you wake up.

Ladies, know your man's trigger. If he's sensitive about the size of his ummm…head, don't ridicule his little… I mean don't talk about the size of his head. Some of you like to get beatings and if you're one of those just ignore this chapter. But if you're one of those that got knocked out and didn't see it coming I might be able to help you with just a few little lessons.

Sometimes a man can make you so mad that you just want to blow up or blow him up. So we scream and scream and scream until we notice that he couldn't care less. Then we get really angry. That's when we go for the jugular. We target all his weak points and we pounce.

"I don't know why I'm with you. I can do sooooooo much better. My people can't believe I'm with you. Yo people can't believe I'm with you. You stupid, low IQ, no job having, Xbox playing mutha.... You ain't nothing but a little beeeeotch, you and yo Momma! What a waste of skin you sorry excuse for a man...and oh yeah, yeah I slept with yo cousin Tyrone and Pookie too. You make me sick with yo little..."

Then.........POW!!!!! You wake up and yo stupid self wondering why he hit you...*ahhhhhhhhhhhhhhhhhhhhhhh!!!*

- Lesson #1: never push your man's buttons while you're within his reach.
- Lesson #2: never talk about a man's Momma, especially a black man's. He will hurt you bad. Some men can stand everything but you talking about their mother.

You get so angry that you can't make him feel as bad as he made you feel that you just have to push that mommy button. Even though you know it might get you killed you're so mad you push it anyway. You've tried everything else to hurt his feelings but nothing else worked. So ladies if you just have to hurt his feelings and talk about his mother, remember lesson#1 and do it from your car. Go get in the car like you just have to leave and start the car up. Roll down the window say what you will and go. I mean go! Go quickly!

- Lesson #3: resist criticizing your man's body. Most men hate it when you ridicule there private parts.

For some reason a lot of men seem to be insecure about their body no matter how well endowed. So when you ridicule them they seem to go into a rage a lot of times causing them to do things that they'll regret later.

Remember he is your man. Respect him as such. Words do hurt and you can't take them back.

- Lesson #4: do not trash or destroy his favorite things or his beautiful car.

This is a hard one to resist but try. You know this is the first thing you want to do and sooooooo many women do it. You destroy his stereo, the speakers and his CDs. You pour bleach into the fish tank and water into his computer and then for the big finish, the car. This is where it gets sticky. Depending on what he drives this stunt could land you in the hospital or worse. If you trash his clunker-mobile you might get away with it if you stay away long enough for him to cool off. But if you trash his Escalade, Jag, Benz, vintage car etc…God help you because I can't. I don't even want to help you.

Another thing that drives some men crazy is spit. Yuck! I have a brother that can't stand to be spat on. He will beat you half to death if you spit on him and again I can't blame him. That's so nasty.

Now ladies sometimes we just go entirely too far. I know women who get mad and harass the man on his job and when he gets fired they have the nerve to look for child support. Stop it! Just stop it because when he gets fired and show-up at your house ready to slap you down, *now yo stupid self* has to get a restraining order. Then you start missing him and want to patch things up. You find some lame excuse to ask him over to the house. One thing leads to another (because you planned it that way) and he moves back in. You forgot all about the restraining order until the two of you starting fighting again. Then you want him out. You want to call the police but he'll tell them that you invited him in. So now you have to pay money to have the order removed. Then you get it put back on and you play this game of on and off for the next few years until the judges get fed up. My friend got so many restraining orders put on her husband that the judge told her the next time she allows her husband to come to the house he was going to arrest her. How embarrassing.

Chapter 12

Where to Find a Man

I hear so many women say that they can't find a man. Their friends tell them that they are looking in the wrong spots. Okay first of all there is no such thing as the wrong spot.

Where can you find a man? Men are all over the place. You can find them in the clubs, supermarkets, Laundromats, barbershops, airports, at work, and in the streets. They go just about every place you do. If you would pay more attention and quit whining about the one you can't get, you'll be amazed at how many single men are out there. My German cousin Martina once told me that German women have a saying, "Other mothers had sons." Yes, men are everywhere. So if you're looking for a man you must be alert. You must be conscious and aware of your surroundings at all times.

When you see a guy you find attractive or interesting approach him and start a conversation. It doesn't matter what you say as long as you say something. Just start with "Hi how are you?" If he's not attracted to you at all and assuming he's not a pig, he'll be polite speak back then turn away. Be observant, if he says more than a few words try to keep the conversation going. If this is a person you bump into regularly make a point to be where he is as often as possible.

Just about everyone has a routine even if they don't know it. Don't mistake routine with being organized. You can be completely disorganized and yet you still have a routine. If you're interested in a man, find out his routine. If there's a place he frequents, you need to be there. Now ladies, be careful, don't stalk him. Men frighten easily. Just pick one place. Don't show up at his church, his job, his gym, his favorite club and his supermarket. Just pick one. If he coaches little league go to the games even if you have to borrow somebody's child. And speaking of borrowing somebody's child, this is a great idea to get you into the barbershop. If you don't have a little boy of your own borrow one, you won't be sorry. You can often find the most gorgeous men at the barbershop, I mean coming and going. Yep, yep! Another idea to get you in if you wear your hair short let a barber fade your cut or line you up. Why make an appointment with the salon just to get lined-up? Most barbers can line you up with their eyes closed and it's probably cheaper and a whole lot more fun. So what you leave smelling like men's cologne, tee-hee you'll probably leave with a date.

Now you've heard the saying, "Don't be shy." Well it's all right to be shy. Shy just means timid and timid means hesitant, cautious, careful or slow to do. So be "slow to do" as long as you "do."

People say the wrong place to meet a man is at a club, humm... That doesn't really make sense to me since most people have gone to parties or clubs. Some nice people like to go out every now and then just to have a little fun. I know a lot of people who met their soul mate at a club. Just remember sisters, be a lady at all times. If you're dressed like a whore you'll be treated like a whore. When your booty is showing some fool will touch it. When your breasts are hanging out some fool will try to touch them. Yeah, I hear you saying, "Just because I dress like this it doesn't give him the right to touch." And you're right but the reality is, if you don't respect yourself no one else will. You can fuss and gripe all you want but I find this to be true, act like a lady and you'll be treated like one.

A lady should never have to spend much money at the club.

When one of my nieces lived with me she had me to hold on to her money so that she wouldn't spend it frivolously. She had a good job and made good money. On her payday she would cash her check and bring the money straight to me at which time I would give her, her two-week allotment. Occasionally she would run out of money.

One day she decided to ask me for some of her money so that she could go out to the club. I laughed and gave her five dollars. "Five dollars!" she screamed. "Auntie what am I going to do with five dollars?" I told her there is no cover charge at the door so you don't need any money to get in and if a woman has to pay for more than one drink she is too ugly (inside or out) to go clubbing, (and I'm not sorry to say, everyone of my nieces is a "whole dime"). I personally have never had to buy myself a drink or a meal in my entire life. She laughed, took the five dollars and went on her way. When she came home later that night she brought me back the five dollars. I laughed and said,

"I told you so." You see you don't have to be a gold digger, just a lady.

Now if the club scene is not for you there are many other places you can try but you must get out of the house. You'll never find a man sitting at home. Don't eat lunch at work go out at lunchtime. Take yourself out to dinner, go to a stage play and by all means flirt, flirt, flirt!

If you lead an active life you'll want a partner that does the same. Know your objective. If your objective is a rich husband, get dressed in your nice clothes and jewelry, grab your knock-off Louis Vuitton and go shopping for expensive cars. You're not actually shopping to buy a car; you're really shopping for a rich-man. Go to every dealership in the city. Flirt with your fellow shoppers and ladies get his advice on which car is the best. He would love to spend hours telling you what he knows about cars.

If you like "Billy the Body Builder", join a gym. If you like religious men, go to church. If you like *um young* go back to college. And if you like bad boys, the jails are full, *(not recommended)* but there's somebody for everybody. People make mistakes and I know of some nice people in prison but please, please, please be-careful.

Another great place to find a man is …wait, wait… wait for it….funerals, yep, yep or better yet the wake!

I have seen the finest mix of men at funeral homes. You will meet more men at funerals than weddings. Men don't particularly like weddings but they will usually pay their last respects to a loved one or a fallen friend and this is a time when you get to see how they really clean-up. When you see one you like inquire about him. Ask everyone you know until you find someone who knows him. Again find out his routine. If there's a place he frequents, you need to be there.

One important question that you should ask first is, IS HE MARRIED? I learned this the hard way. I was at a wedding and I saw a fine dude. I mean he was fine! I was with my little sister and my best friend. Hired to shoot the wedding, I followed this guy all around the reception hall trying to get his picture. My sis and friend were laughing hysterically. Every time I tried to take the guy's picture he would get up and move to the other side of this very large reception hall. I was in one of my bold flirtatious moods so I totally ignored the fact that he was with a woman who I felt couldn't possibly be his wife. I mean it never even crossed my mind. For real! Even when my friend said, "That's probably his woman." I said, "nah" and after all I just wanted to flirt for the night. He continued to elude me until he went to the men's room. Finally, I had him cornered. I sat outside the door waiting with my cohorts. When he came out of the bathroom I raised my camera and asked him to smile. I thanked him and as he walked away I said "umph umph umph you're the finest man in the place." I continued to flirt harmlessly through out the evening thankful that his companion was busy helping with the reception. A few days later when I delivered the wedding photos to the bride I told her of my flirtatious escapades with the fine man describing him from head to toe. Instantly she knew who I was describing. "That's my cousin she said and the heavy set woman was his wife." I was immediately sick to my stomach. Oh my God I was coming on to a married man. That was so not cool. I wanted to die but I learned a valuable lesson. Now I know to find out if the man is married first.

So, is it okay to sweat a guy? Definitely, some guys are worth the risk. What are the risks you say? You risk being embarrassed and feeling humiliated. The guy may brag to his boys of how you blow up his cell phone or how you chase him down but if he's all you can think about morning, noon and night than he's worth the risk. And if you end up getting embarrassed, you will get over it. But you might end up with the man of your dreams and everyone else's. Some times you have to take a chance, "nothing ventured, nothing gained".

Chapter 13

Keep Him or Kick Him

Age brings about a change in more ways than one. As they say you live and you learn. When I was younger I said if a guy cheats on you he doesn't love you. As time went on I realized that it's just not that cut and dry. I even had a slogan, *"I don't put up with cheating or beating but I'll take a beating before I put up with cheating"*. Hee, hee, I mean I lived by this. I thought that all women who forgave their man were weak and stupid. After all, if he cheats on you once he'll cheat on you again right…ummmmmmm…maybe. Life doesn't come with guarantees. The question is how much do you love him and is the relationship worth saving. Okay so I have to admit I was a little slow learning this but better late than never and luckily I've suffered no real damage.

My mother laughs because my nieces always call me for relationship advice. One of my nieces called me and my mom asked "what did your niece want"?

I told her you know… she got man problems.

My mother cracked-up. "Why they call you? You don't know nothing about men."

Then I cracked-up. "I know hun? But you know what, I give good advice because I know how to treat people and I know how I want to be treated. I also know that the only perfection God expects from us is spiritual perfection so this fleshly body is subject to error.

When it comes to giving relationship advice I try to keep it simple. That "do unto others thing" seems to work pretty good as well as "walking in the other person's shoes."

When giving relationship advice I also try to keep it as positive as possible. I practice to never say girl leave him because I don't want to be responsible for your lonely nights. You shouldn't listen to people who tell you to leave your mate. This should be your choice. I always say you'll know when you've had enough. Now there are a few of you who just don't catch on but most of you will know (see chapter 14).

Sooooo… if your man cheats on you does he still love you? Hummm? Put it this way. I'll say just because your man cheated on you doesn't mean that he doesn't love you. Some men are just weak and those whores out there can do some amazing things to get your man. That's why men shouldn't put themselves in sticky situations.

Now weather you choose to forgive him or not is entirely up to you but a very wise woman once told me, "you don't let no woman walk off with your man". I ain't going to let some woman just take my man. So you have to ask yourself a question, is he worth fighting for? Now if he's just a boyfriend and there's not a whole lot invested in the relationship gurrrrrrl I say get you another one but if he's your husband that's a different story. And if you still love him, (boyfriend or husband) fight, fight, fight. Now when I say fight I don't mean for you to beat that hoe's …………um, um you know. I mean fight for your marriage.

I think that most men (*caring men*) who cheat are victims of circumstances (most), always in the wrong place at the wrong time and get caught-up. Ladies don't throw away years of commitment because some hoe seduced your man one night. Now if he continues to do it, well like I said you should know when enough is enough.

There is one thing that is hard for me to accept. That is when he has a mistress. A mistress is the other woman who he spends time with and has just as committed a relationship with her as he does with you. Ooh that's hard. He has a toothbrush at your house he has a toothbrush at her house. He has clothes at your house he has clothes at her house. He has kids at your house and he has a baby at her house. Yeah, this is the woman that gets pregnant and stakes an eighteen year claim on your man and y'all moneys. Now my hat's off to the women who can hold their relationship together after that but I don't think I can do it. Again I'm being careful. I'm not saying that I won't do it because I don't want to have to eat crow but Lord please don't give me that test.

So if your husband has a mistress, you need to do some hard soul searching. Are you doing your part in the relationship? Are you feeding his needs physically and emotionally? Examine yourself and if you're doing your part you might want to kick him to the curb. Remember “Other mothers had sons”. But if you just want your husband no matter what, then keep him, after all he is yours. You have the rights to him the other woman doesn’t. And don’t let anybody shame you or make you feel embarrassed. Your friends will call you a fool, say you’re stupid and talk about you behind your back but he’s yours, yours…yours, yours and yours. Maybe he fills your needs. They can’t! So don’t listen to them. As a matter of fact don’t talk about your man’s faults to your girlfriends, not even your best friend. A lot of times that’s the friend that ends up sleeping with your man. And stay away from those nice guys; (Mr. Understanding) you know the ones who we feel we can talk to. He’s just so nice and understanding. That’s the guy you’ll end up sleeping with.

I think a person should leave before they cheat. A lot of women cheat because their man doesn’t give them attention anymore. Boy oh boy that’s when we meet Mr. Understanding.

Sometimes a relationship has just run its course and it’s just over. There are signs that let you know that you’re ready to move on. Here are a few:

- He’s not funny anymore.

Remember when you use to laugh at everything he said, now he just annoying?

- You’re uncomfortable being alone with him.

You use to love being alone with him. One of the biggest problems you had was trying to find time that the two of you could spend together alone.

- Your friends and family are uncomfortable around you two.

Your bad relationship is so obvious that you make everyone around you feel nervous.

- The sight of him makes you sick.

Remember when he used to be sooooooo fine? His voice once sexy and deep now sounds repulsive and robotic. The smile that once lit-up the room now looks silly and that infectious, roaring laugh now sounds like an annoying laughing hyena. You once thought of him as chocolate and velvety now he just black and crusty.

- You start reminiscing about your ex-boyfriends.

"Why oh why did I let him get away? I should've married so-and-so". You've forgotten all the bad things that "*so-and-so*" did to you or those things just don't seem so bad anymore.

- You don't care how you look around him.

I love my mother she's seventy one years old and she's beautiful. She has health problems right now but she could still pass for about fifty seven, fifty eight. And boy does she care about the way she looks. Now she needs to write a book about how to treat a man. I may not agree with all her ways but the only thing she could be accused of is treating them too well.

She could teach us a thing or two about how to keep a man because she's kept one for over fifty three years. Do you know that till this day she doesn't want my father to see her looking bad (yes they're still together)? She says that a woman should be up, dressed, hair combed, looking and smelling good by the time her man gets up.

Remember when you wouldn't be caught dead looking bad in front of him? Now you couldn't care less.

Relationships are hard work. Last time I checked the divorce rate, fifty percent of first marriages, sixty seven percent of second marriages and seventy four percent of third marriages ended in divorce.

Chapter 14

He Doesn't Want You

I think that some women are just stuck on stupid. If your man starts to complain too much about your looks and pointing out your weight gain every chance he gets, chances are he doesn't want you anymore. There are signs that tell you when a man doesn't want you. Everything you do or say aggravates him and he starts knit-picking arguments so he can have an excuse to leave the house. He stays out late or doesn't come home until the next day. He never talks to you anymore but he seems to have plenty of things to talk about to the person on the other end of the cell phone. And speaking of that, why does he have to take the call in the bathroom? He shows you no affection what so ever and he'd rather hang out with the boys than touch you.

If a man doesn't want you he will give you signs. They are cowards and hate to just walk away from the relationship so they try to make you miserable so that you'll leave. The problem is women are long suffering creatures. A lot of women will ignore the signs hoping that they'll go away. In some cases the man will turn around and say, "What am I doing. I got a good woman." But in most cases he will get worse, cheat on you incessantly and make your life miserable until you wake up and realize that he doesn't want you anymore.

I think it's better for a woman if she reads the signs and moves on with her life and of course the sooner the better.

Every situation is different and you need to figure out why his feelings have changed towards you and can you fix it. Maybe you're neglecting him and his needs? Or maybe you've just become so boring that he's about to lose his mind. Have you gained or lost an enormous amount of weight? People say that your mate should love you for who you are but that's only partly true. He may still love you but just no longer find you attractive. It's great when we find that jewel of a man who says "Honey I will still love you when your hair turns gray and if you get as fat as a bail of hay. And there are some men like that (these are real men). But it's not fair to say that the men who don't feel the same way are bad. I'm not saying that they're good but let's be realistic, we are human beings not angles. We are tied to this flesh and when we pick our mates we are usually attracted to the whole creature, spirit, mind, and BODY.

I once knew a young woman who we'll call Jane, newly separated from her husband Dick (don't laugh y'all, pun NOT intended). She was a very pretty young lady, "light skin-did-did", long gorgeous hair, with ample hips. She began telling me the story of how she and her husband got together, how everyone wanted him and he chose her. She was in her first year of college at a prestigious university and he was impressed. But before a year of marriage had passed he began to verbalize how unhappy he was with the marriage and that he felt they should take a small break from each other.

No I don't think so she told him and she refused to leave, knowing that the only place she could go was back to her hometown and her parent's house. After a few more weeks or so he asked her if she would please leave for a little while and give him a little break and once more she refused. Soon after that he asked yet again and this time she agreed to leave.

While on her own, Jane realized that she needed to learn how to be a little more independent. Having already flunked out of college she got a job working hard and began to lose weight including those ample hips. The long hair was also work so she cut it completely off. I mean her hair was so short she could barely get it around the smallest hair roller.

As time went on Dick began to miss Jane and asked her to come home. Excited, Jane packed her belongings and returned home to her husband. But just as she began to get comfortable at home he came home with a bus ticket for her to return to her parent's house.

Jane tried to hide her shock as she once again packed her things.

As I listened to her story I just couldn't understand why he was so displeased with her after such a short period of time until I learned more about him.

He was a somewhat characteristic black man who liked smart yet light complexioned black women with long hair and big butts. You see Jane was not the person Dick thought she was. She wasn't as smart as the prestigious college she attended led him to believe and this for him became an intellectual problem. But she still had the physical attributes that he loved right? Wrong! The long hair that once hung down her back was gone and she was now a slim size five with no hips. All that was left was the light skin.

Now don't be mad at Dick. He wasn't really a bad guy; he just made the mistake of marring Jane before he really knew her. He was forthcoming and honest telling her to leave and yet he did not have the courage to tell her why. Some guys are subtle at first but if you don't catch the hint they will become increasingly rude.

Pay attention, something might be wrong if your man is away more nights than he is home. Something's wrong when you have to walk home in the dark because he too lazy to pick you up from work. Check it out, something's wrong when he has PMS more than you do. He won't help you carry the groceries in the house but he helps Lolita next door. Be diligent and read the signs which may include:

1. Too tired for sex.
2. He doesn't come home at night.
3. He doesn't call unless he wants something.
4. He lies!
5. He picks fights.
6. Everything you do is wrong.
7. Everything you like is stupid.

8. He lies!!
9. He looks guilty all the time.
10. His boys look guilty around you.
11. He's never where you are.
12. He lies!!!
13. His answer to every question is "Whatever" or "I don't care".
14. He doesn't care what time you come home.
15. He never shows any signs of affection.
16. He's secretive and He lies!!!!

Chapter 15

Heal a Broken Heart

He was the one, tall dark and handsome. He was the first thing on your mind when you woke up and the last voice you wanted to hear before you went to bed, and you loved him. He was your soul mate. Nothing could break you up…you thought. Then you caught him with Judy. Now you're sick. You cry everyday. You don't want to go out with your friends and you either got your hair in a ponytail, combed straight back or you got a baseball cap on your head. Fast forward three months later. You've gained twenty pounds and you're cursing yourself. You passed him on the streets he's looking good and you're looking a mess! Get a grip. Don't you know that your weakness empowers him?

Your broken heart will heal but how long it takes is up to you. It's okay to cry. As a matter of fact you should cry your heart out. It helps in the healing.

But please don't let him see you. Don't let anybody see you but your closest friend and confidant. When you break-up with a guy that you loved, it's like experiencing death and with death comes grief. Therefore there are five stages of grief you must get through; Denial, Anger, Bargaining, Depression and finally Acceptance.

You will spend the first few weeks thinking that you'll get back together. He just needs some space. That's denial. You show up at his place. You just wanted to return something to him. You know, any excuse to see him. You talk, you stay too long and you end up doing something that you should not have done. Now you lay, smiling triumphed and relaxed. That is until he nudges you and says, Rita get up, you got to go before Judy gets home. Then you realize that's he's gone for good and you move on to the second stage, Anger.

Ahhhhhhh, anger! This is the stage where you put dog poop in his mailbox, key his car, slash his tires and break the windshield and headlights out. This is the phase where you spray paint his white car red and his black car yellow. This is the time when you egg his car and steal the license plate, super glue the doors and the gas tank flap shut, put bologna and birdseeds on his hood and watch the birds do their thing. You subscribe for Ladies Home Journal and Gay Men's Magazine in his name and when all these things fail to satisfy that's when you start making prank phone calls to Judy and threatening her with bodily harm. When your anger has completely exhausted you and you get out of jail you enter into what is called the bargaining stage.

Stage three; you call your ex just to apologize. *"I know I was tripping"*, you confess *"but it's just that I love you so much. If you take me back I'll be a better girlfriend. I'll wash your clothes and cook your meals, I'll let you hang out with your boys and I'll even do that thing that you've been asking me to do. Please, please, please! Please take me back. Hello...hello..."*

When you realize that you have degraded yourself over and over again depression begins to set in. Congratulations! You've reached stage four. This is when you stop combing your hair and going out with your friends. You either gain weight from eating everything in sight trying to fill that empty feeling or you can't eat and you lose so much weight you start to look like a crack-head fiend. You feel hopeless and care very little about your future. You cry continuously and your whole world seems dark. But it will get better you will get over him eventually.

The key is to avoid him. Don't go to places that you frequented as a couple. Do not call him when you get the urge to and when you can't stop thinking about him, concentrate on the bad times and the hurt he inflicted on your emotions. Think about how he clowned you in front of his boys and embarrassed you in front of your girls. Remember how he chewed with his mouth open, smacked his food, burped all through dinner and farted all through the night. But most of all don't forget he left you for Judy.

Occupy your time with positive things. Hang out with positive people and don't accept invitations to pity parties from your negative friends. If you're not careful you will find yourself hanging out with the Bitter Biddies. You know the man bashers. Don't act like you don't know, we've all been a Bitter

Biddy at some time in our life. The problem with this is that it doesn't make you feel better. You all sit around the room telling each other what some no good nigg… I mean man did to you. Someone tells the story about how their husband got up early every morning to go to a job that he didn't have. One day the alarm didn't go off and he woke up frantic and cussing about being late. I've had at least three women tell me this story. The stories are usually funny when you're telling them but they have a backlash effect when you get home alone and re-hatch them.

Doing volunteer work for the elderly or disabled can also help. It's hard to be sad when you're helping others. Go to a basketball game or football or baseball whatever floats your boat but let it be a sport with nice *young men*, bwaaaaaaah. Okay, that's just me. But do something new, you get the picture. Time will heal your broken heart and bring you to the final stage of grief, Acceptance.

There are things that you will be tempted to try that will not heal a broken heart.

1. Liquor – Some women turn to liquor but the drunk wears off. I've never drank so I can't tell you how it feels but I can tell you how you look. You look stupid. I got a cousin who loves to "get her drink on". She's funny about who she drinks with because she says "I ain't about that drunk S" (now S don't stand for stuff cause she cusses). She says getting drunk makes you do un-lady like things that you'll forget you did in the morning.

2. Pills – Other women turn to pills but the high wears off and the more you take the more you need until you reach a threshold. The next step is an overdose.

3. Junk Food – Junk food leads to weight gain and weight gain creates more problems. See now we're talking my expertise. Junk food is my solution to every problem. If I'm sad I eat junk food, mad, junk food, depressed, junk food, lonely, junk food, horny, junk food, you get the picture. Don't do that. Losing weight is one of the hardest things there is to do.

4. Screwing his friends or just plain hoeing – you just degrade yourself and he's even happier he dumped you.

Now, what you should do is get back to dating. Don't try to find a new boyfriend. You need some time to heal and if you're not healed, if you're still wounded you take that wound into your new relationship sometimes dooming it from the start. So just date. Date anybody, date everybody. Just date. Don't hoe, date!

Chapter 16

Home Remedies

Some people say that I look younger than I am; well I try to do some of the things that the old folks recommended. Sometimes I can't. Say for instance eating garlic. They say garlic is a miracle cure for what ails you but I just can't eat it. Apple Cider Vinegar (natural cider vinegar not that grocery store stuff) is the other miracle. It's one of the best home remedies for everything from obesity to acid reflux.

I love home remedies. Thank God for old people. We need to keep up with the old home remedies that our grandparents used. Here are some remedies that I remember and found useful. I've also included a lot that other people have told me about down thru the years including my doctors.

Acne - Mix one teaspoon of lemon juice with one teaspoon of finely-ground cinnamon and apply on affected areas frequently. This will help with the acne and the lemon juice will also fade the dark spots that acne usually leaves behind.

Lemon juice is a natural bleaching agent so when you have discoloration on any part of your body, think lemon juice.

Anemia - Drink eight ounces of apple juice on an empty stomach before going to bed.

Appetite Suppressant – Suck on eucalyptus cough drops. It has a numbing effect.

Arthritis - Slice a medium sized potato in a cup of water and let set overnight drink first thing in the morning. Wow the old folks really could come up with some things. But it's easy to give it a try.

Athlete's foot - Soak feet in a tub of hot water (not burning hot) mix in one half cup of vinegar and two tablespoons of baking soda. Soak for a half hour then dry thoroughly.

Bacterial Vaginitis – Apply plain yogurt directly into the vagina.

Bad Breath – Rinse mouth with peroxide diluted with water. Sip a glass of water with lemon juice added.

Baldness – Eat a handful of white sesame seeds every morning. Hee-hee, I wonder if this works.

Bedwetting - Eat two walnut halves and a teaspoon of raisins before going to bed.

Bites (insect) – Apply chlorine bleach with a q-tip.

Black Eye – A semi frozen steak is the best remedy or so I'm told. They say it's the vitamins in the meat. Also as soon as the injury occurs, placing an ice pack over your eye for at least one hour will prevent the black eye from ever materializing.

Bleeding Gums – Brush teeth with anti bacteria soap instead of toothpaste.

Blisters - Aloe Vera, vitamin E oil, or zinc ointment will help heal a blister.

Body Odor – Add a cup or two of vinegar to your bath and soak, soak, soak. This keeps you feeling fresh all day.

Boils - Apply hot cabbage leafs or onions (room temp) externally on boils which helps to draw out infection and/or ripen them, pop the boil and withdraw the pus.

Bruises - Apply apple cider vinegar to the bruise followed by an ice pack.

Burning tongue - I've had this all my life especially around my cycle. It's brought on a lot of times by stress. Eat foods high in vitamin B like whole grains, oats, barley, wheat bran, yeast, avocado, lentils, leafy greens, salmon and nuts.

Burns – Run ice cold water over burned area for ten to fifteen minutes. Also try coating affected area in egg white. While the egg white is still wet you should feel no pain from the burn. As soon as it dries up the pain comes back so reapplication is necessary. This method not only alleviates the pain it actually heals and prevents scarring from the burn. If you burn your tongue, immediately place a teaspoon of sugar into your mouth. Let the sugar sit on your tongue until it dissolves.

Another burn remedy is Vick's Vapor Rub. Apply Vick's to the burn area immediately and the pain should subside and the burn will heal nicely.

Chapped Lips – I like Vaseline mixed with a little bit of honey and your man won't be mad at you either. You can also tint it with just a little bit of color using your favorite lipstick.

Common Cold – Chicken soup! Yep, grandma knew. Also try lemon and honey tea.

Constipation – Lettuce works best to me, but also apple, raisins, prunes and oh yes my favorite, watermelon.

Corns - Put banana peels on the wart and bandage. Repeat every night before you go to bed.

Cough – For dry cough, soak some almonds in a glass of warm water overnight. Remove the skins and grind into a paste with a little margarine and sugar. Take as needed for dry cough. For congested cough mix five tablespoons of honey with equal parts cider vinegar and warm water. Take one tablespoon as needed.

Dark Skin or Hyperpigmentation - Again lemon or lime juice.

Dark underarms - To remedy most skin discoloration use lemon juice.

Depression – Try drinking two cups of ginger tea a day. Unfortunately ice cream is also good for depression (use with caution).

Diaper Rash - Corn starch is great and if you don't have any cornstarch then brown some dry flour on in a pan on the stove let cool and use like baby powder.

Diarrhea – My Auntie used to put a teaspoon of flour in a glass of water. I could never get it down but they say it works.

Ear infection - Every since I could remember my folks used Hydrogen peroxide for ear aches and infections.

Eczema - Apply honey to the affected area. Honey is a natural antibiotic.

Edema - Eat brown rice at least twice a week.

Fever- Soak the sole of a pair of white cotton socks in egg whites and put them on the patient's feet. Make sure to put a pad under the feet to keep the bed dry. Watch the fever fall.

Flu – Get plenty of rest and drink hot lemon and honey tea. Remember honey is a natural antibiotic and is rich in antioxidants.

Gas – Simple, just put a little vinegar in a small glass of water and drink.

Gingivitis -Again use diluted peroxide as your mouthwash.

Hair Degreaser – Instead of shampoo use dish detergent at lease once a month or whenever you have used greasy hair products.

Halitosis - Brush your teeth with baking soda. Swallow one tablespoon of apple cider vinegar before each meal. Drink chamomile tea.

Hangover –I've never had one but they say for breakfast eat two oranges sprinkled with salt, or drink a large glass of orange juice with a pinch of salt added.

Headache – Stand under a hot shower and let the water ease the headache away. This even helps migraines. A lot of times it won't work on black women because we refuse to get our hair wet, bwaaaaaaah.

Heartburn, Indigestion and Vomiting – Now, this has saved my life more than I care to think about. Mix two tablespoons of vinegar, a half teaspoon of baking soda and six ounces of water in a large glass. Stir quickly. The concoction will foam like seltzer so please remember to use a large glass. Drink down immediately for instant relief. I said instant relief.

Hemorrhoids - Wash the area with warm water. Saturate gauze, cotton or tissue with witch-hazel. Place it on the hemorrhoids for about an hour then apply some castor oil. Ahh, what a relief it is.

Hiccups – Slowly swallowing a teaspoonful of sugar can eliminate the hiccups.

High Cholesterol - One teaspoon of honey and one teaspoon of lime juice in one cup of hot water and drink early morning. Eat plenty of bran.

High Blood Pressure – My mom says to eat garlic and several other people agree but *I ain't gon be able to do it*. I just don't like garlic but it is really good for you. Parsley tea is also an old home remedy.

Insomnia – Sex, sex, sex! Bwaaaaaaah! Whud? That's what my lil sister told me. Okay, okay. Try warm milk. I hated it when I was a kid but I really like it now. They say add a little honey but sometimes I like to add a little ice cream. If none of this suits your fancy try chamomile tea. Hot showers or warm baths also work. On hot days try cool showers right before bed. The change in body temperature can sometimes be exhausting resulting in a good night's sleep.

Jaundice - I have heard of many treatments for jaundice but to me the easiest is to drink plenty of tomato juice and lemon or lime water daily.

Please note (jaundice is a sign of a more serious problem and you should seek medical attention.)

Menopause – Cinnamon has been known to help women get through the many perils of menopause. So eat it on your cereal, toast, cakes and pies. Drink it in your teas hot or cold. Sprinkle it everywhere. Be creative. Also soy milk or supplements.

Menstrual Cramps – My Aunt told me years ago to drink ginger tea. Fresh pounded ginger is best steeped into a tea and sweetened to taste. Drink three times a day.

Morning Sickness – Ice or popsicles.

Obesity - Eat raw cabbage it stops the conversion of sugar into fat.

Osteoporosis - Eat sesame seeds daily and drink dandelion tea to help build bone density.

Nausea – Soda cracker I find works the best plus ginger ale and again Popsicles and also popcorn.

Nosebleed - Pinch the soft part of nose with your thumb and index finger for five to ten minutes. Place an ice pack between the eyes.

Palpitation - Roll and squeeze a lemon until it's soft. Cut the tip off and insert a heaping teaspoonful of honey. Mix it inside the lemon with the end of the spoon or a dull butter knife then suck the juice from the lemon. Grape juice has also been said to ease heart palpitations.

PMS – Try eating lettuce salad for constipation and water retention and ice cream for the mood swings. Also try hot chamomile or lemon tea with a tablespoon of whiskey (they said **one** tablespoon).

Scarring – To prevent scarring apply a fresh banana peel to your injury. Wrap the injury or place a large band-aid over the spot, which ever works best. Repeat daily until satisfied.

Sinus – One tablespoon of natural apple cider vinegar every night before going to bed.

Sore Throat – You should add ¼ teaspoon of cayenne pepper to a cup of warm water or coffee and drink slowly stirring occasionally if needed. I find this distasteful so I recommend adding the cayenne pepper to a cup of veggie soup or hot V8.

Stings - Apply mud to the sting or apply honey immediately after being stung by a bee.

Stress – Try drinking herbal teas like sage or chamomile also ice cream in moderation.

Sweating – Sage tea. Try making the tea from fresh sage leaves. When using herbal teas for medicinal purposes always use fresh herbs.

Toe nail fungus - Soak your nails in warm bleach water, rinse and apply tea tree oil.

Toothache - Apply clove oil to the gum surrounding the bad tooth with a q-tip.

Wrinkles - Apply egg whites under your eyes and use castor oil for moisturizer.

Yeast Infections - Eat plenty of plain yogurt. If you're prone to yeast infections eating plain yogurt can help with the problem. Do not eat yogurt with fruit added.

Zoster (Herpes) or as we call it Chicken Pox – This is not a cure, we all know the drill but backing soda baths will help you through.

Chapter 17

Random Thoughts

So I've tried to tell you of all the topics that my nieces have come to me with over the years but they seem to be endless. So hear are a few more that came to my mind. Even though they deserve their own chapter, I mean seriously who has that kind of time. So as different subjects came to my mind whether I was watching TV, having dinner or having a conversation with my nieces, I would jot them down on a list.

I couldn't figure out how to list them by importance so I just put them in alphabetical order.

Baby Daddy and Baby Momma Drama – This topic has everything to do with respect. I'm not a baby momma and I don't have a man that's a baby daddy but boy have I seen my share of baby momma drama.

Women know they use their children to hurt or get even with their ex-husbands or boyfriends. If the man loves his child I mean really loves his baby, he's in trouble. His ex will use the baby to no end. Every time he turns around there's an ultimatum in his face. Ladies, don't do that. That's just selfish. Why rob your child of a father? You're just being stupid. Don't you know that a baby daddy who wants to see his child is a free babysitter? Get over yourself and let that man see his child.

Why is it that you won't let Lil Johnny spend the night with his daddy now that his daddy has a new girl friend? You don't want the man but you're pissed that he has a new girl. So you say "Johnny can't go over your house anymore cause I don't know her." You try to plead your case to your friends and family but you're just wrong. You don't see it until you're the other woman and you're mad because some ignorant chick won't let your man see his kids why, because she don't know you! "I don't know her" you screamed. But now the shoe is on the other foot, your new boyfriend is having the same problem. His ex won't let him see his kids and you call her a dirty witch or that other word that rhyme with witch. You're so upset that the woman won't let your man see his kids that you forgot that you did the same thing to your ex.

Now y'all know I'm a firm believer in child support but child support is not a revenge tool. Up the child support when you need the support not because he got married to Miss America and you got stretch marks. Ladies; you need to get it together.

Okay now men y'all got some mess with y'all too. Visiting hours are not one, two or three o'clock in the morning. Ladies stop letting your baby daddy show up at your house at midnight pretending that they want to see their child. You know the real reason he comes late at night is to give you another baby. He knows the baby is sleep. Let the baby sleep and as for you…WAKE UP!

Child Support – First of all we need to define the meaning of child support. To all the fathers or sperm contributors out there, child support is not your baby's money. It is money given to your ex-spouse, ex-girlfriend, concubine or baby momma to help pay living expenses to feed, house and clothe your child. Like it or not the money is not your child's but its mother. Pay attention ladies it's your money. And for every woman out there who doesn't press child support you are guilty of child abuse unless you have a substantial income and really, I mean really don't need the money. When you don't press child support because you feel sorry for the man and your child who by the way didn't ask to be born has to go without, you are guilty of negligence. What kind of woman neglects her child because she feels sorry for the man who left her with the child? Some women don't press support because they think that the man will one day come back to them and they don't want to make him mad. You're a fool. Other women say "I don't want nothing from him" and guess what you're a fool too. It ain't about you! It's about the child and the child having everything they need to make life easier already being deprived of a father in the home. And what you do with the money is nobodies business weather you buy GEICO or Lipo just as long as the child is being well taken care of. Shoot, a little Lipo might land you a better job and you might not need his child support (hee hee). But seriously, when you don't press child support, every time your child needs clothes, shoes, a winter coat, a hair cut, a special tutor, braces, glasses or school supplies and you have to keep putting it off till you can afford it, you are guilty of child abuse.

Ex-Cons – We all got them in our families. Some of the best men I've ever known were ex-convicts. Being an ex-con doesn't mean that the person is a bad person it just means that they did something illegal, got caught and convicted. Notice I said got caught. Everyone in this world would be an ex-con if only we got caught. Yeah, all y'all bootlegging, welfare frauding, cable stealing, self-righteous *ka-riss-tens* are so quick to misjudge people. You know I don't mind being judge, it's being misjudge that bothers me.

So how do we determine which ex-cons are okay? Hum, how about a little common sense.

I started to give some case scenarios but I changed my mind. I couldn't think of one that wouldn't get me in trouble.

Guilt – Guilt is a bad feeling. But if it wasn't for guilt people would do anything and everything they wanted to do without a sense of right and wrong. When you do something wrong you should feel guilty it's called being human, having a conscience. I love when my nieces do something wrong. They look so funny because their faces show their guilt. They always tell me what they did because they just can't hide it. The guilt eats them alive. This is a good thing.

So by now you're thinking why bring up the subject. Because some people just don't know when to let it go. You did something bad and you can't seem to forgive yourself and worse yet someone else won't let you forget it. You should feel terrible, you should feel sorrowful, you should make amends then you should move on. Guilt will drive you crazy. Let it go! You cheated on your mate. That was wrong and hopefully your mate will forgive you but if they never do, you still have to move on. Don't let the situation destroy you.

If you were on bad terms with someone and they died before the two of you could come to terms you should feel sad that the two of you couldn't resolve the problem but that's all. Don't let guilt drive you to your grave. Grieve then move on. It may take a little while before you can move on, that's okay. That just means you have a live conscience. But eventually you must move on and don't let anybody else make you feel bad either. It's okay to forgive yourself. It's the right thing to do. I don't care if you cheated on your spouse, abused your child, lied to your parents, stole from the collection plate, hit the neighbor's cat, killed the neighbor's dog or made a fat girl cry. I'm not saying be cold hearted but eventually you must forgive yourself.

Grief – Did you know that there's no pill for grief? I remember when my baby brother died the doctor gave me Xanax and it put me to sleep. Guess what when I woke up my brother was still dead. I took another Xanax, went to sleep but when I woke up same thing. By the forth day Xanax had no effect and I had to deal with my loss. So it began …the five stages of grief. There's no getting around it you must grieve.

I still wanted a magic pill. I watch TV. Those rich old white ladies were taking something. I wanted that.

Two and a half years later I lost my big sister. So now I have a new doctor Dr. Wright and that's a perfect name for her because she's fabulous. Surely she'll give me something to take away my pain, right? Wrong. Instead she was the one who enlightened me. She said that she could give me something for anxiety and she could give me something for depression but what I was experiencing was grief and grief has to take its course. So I experienced them all; Denial, Anger, Bargaining, Depression and finally Acceptance. Well, I'm still trying to accept it.

Judging – I judge yes I do! When someone tells you stop judging me they're usually doing something wrong. When you're wrong you're wrong and if I tell you you're wrong I'm just telling you the truth. But this is not really judging. Some people will just accuse you of judging them just to get you off their back.

I remember when we used to correct each other and it made us want to be a better person. Now, we see people doing wrong and we just pat them on the back. Nobody's perfect you say.

I say if you're a bad person I'm going to call it like I see it and if that's judging then so be it. I want you to judge me too. You do it anyway. If you have an opinion of someone you had to judge them first to come to an opinion.

Kids – Whoop yo kids! If you don't the cops will.

One day I was catching the bus to church when I met a young woman from Detroit sitting at the bus stop. She asked me where I went to church. When I told her she smiled and said I can't believe it that's where I'm trying to go but I didn't know where it was.

The funny thing is that I never catch the bus to church but I didn't drive at the time and I couldn't find a ride. Well you know what they say "the Lord works in mysterious ways".

As we rode the bus together we began to talk about people who get angry when they see you discipline your children. She told me a story about taking her children to the doctor. She said that she had the "baddest" kids you ever wanted to see. So when her kids began to act up in the doctor's office she spanked them. When she got home the police and Child Services were waiting for her. She couldn't believe it when they told her that she had been reported for abusing her children. She knew right away that the doctor's office had reported her. So the next time she took the kids to the doctor she said she let the kids tear it up.

They turned the office upside down and inside out and when they were finished with that one they wandered into the next office and did more of the same.

"I just sat there, " she said. "Even when they left and went into the other office, I just sat there. The nurse from the other office brought them back and said "whose kids are these?"

I said "mine".

As the lady continued to tell the story I laughed hysterically.

The kids ran through the office again tearing up magazines and turning over chairs. As they reached for a stethoscope the nurse had reached her boiling point. The same nurse that she suspected had called the police on her had snapped, grabbed one child with force and raised her hand to smack him at which time the she stood up and shook her head. "You better not" she said "and get your hands off of him". The doctor came out to see what all the commotion was.

"Lady can't you do something with your kids?"

She said "No, when I did y'all called Child Services".

I loved it. I betcha they never called Child Services on another mother.

My sister once told me a story about a woman who brought her child with her to her job. The child would not behave so the woman tapped the child on his legs a couple of times to settle him down. The workers told my sister to call the cops and my sister being the boss told them no way. She said she told the woman she's doing the right thing and if she really wanted to get him good, take him to the bathroom.

Right on!

Moral Decay – Nobody can deny that this world has suffered moral decay. Things we know are wrong we call right. Nobody thinks twice about an unwed mother it's just okay. Shacking up? Okay! Sleeping with another woman's husband or another man's wife, okay. Well guess what it's still not okay. Parents please, please start teaching your children manners and morals.

Myths – Many of us have grown up with different myths, but which ones should we believe and are some of them true? If you eat Pop Rocks and drink a soda, your stomach will explode and you'll die. Constant knuckle-cracking causes arthritis and coffee stunts your growth. If you touch a toad, you'll get warts, chocolate can cause acne and cats can steal the air from a baby's mouth. I have heard these sayings every since I was a little girl and none of them are true.

They say that if you pull a grey hair out of your head five more will grow back in its place. If this were true I would have all grey hair. I have been pulling out the same five grey hairs for eighteen years.

There're so many old wives tales floating around that it makes it hard some times to distinguish fact from fiction.

Having sex standing up is not a contraceptive and if you picked out your husband by the size of his nose, thumbs and feet, then you'll just have a big nose, big hand, big footed man. Studies found that there is no connection between the size of a man's appendages and the size of his penis.

Puppy Love – Contrary to popular belief, puppy love is still real love. I had my first boyfriend when I was in kindergarten. I made him pies (mud pies) and coconut cake (cakes of mud with grass clippings sprinkled over it). See even then I believed in cooking for my man.

My parents were no-nonsense parents. They were heavy on the morals and my siblings and I followed their rules. When they weren't around our oldest brother and sister were in charge and we gave them the utmost respect. We were not allowed to cuss, smoke, drink, dress provocatively or just hang out. Our parents didn't even want my sister and I to wear make-up or get our ears pierced. But one thing we could always have… was a boyfriend. I remember when I was about ten years old I asked my father if I could have a boyfriend.

He said "yeah, as long as you bring him to the house."

I said for real?

He said "yeah, if I say no you'll sneak around, then I'll have to kill you. I don't want you sneaking around. Just bring him home."

My father is a wise man. My sister and I never did anything to betray our parents trust.

You see puppy love is still love and little kids don't know the difference. They feel the joy and happiness that a relationship brings along with the hurt and sadness that a break-up brings just like adults, albeit on a different level. When forbidden to see each other, couples as young as twelve years old have been known to run away together. Please, please don't tell these children that they don't know what love is. Just be an attentive parent and monitor the relationship.

Psychiatrist - Merriam-Webster's Medical Dictionary defines Psychiatry as; a branch of medicine that deals with the science and practice of treating mental, emotional, or behavioral disorders especially as originating in endogenous causes or resulting from faulty interpersonal relationships. I call it bull crap.

To all the black people who have fallen for this new age awareness, (because black people never use to go to psychiatrist) I feel sorry for you. And I find parents that send their children to psychiatrist are just plain lazy or want to throw the responsibility of raising their kids to somebody else. You don't want to take the time to find out what's bothering your child. So you make the mistake of putting them in the system, big mistake. It follows them through out their entire life. What I hate most about psychiatry is that it is largely based on a European way of thinking. Let's face it people, black people have a totally different way of thinking. Things that we feel are important psychiatrist call ignorant and unlearned. For example I know it's necessary to whip your child but psychiatrist call it barbaric. Why is it that only ethnic or minority beliefs are considered unlearned or ignorant? I'll give psychiatry creditability when it takes in account, studies and embraces my culture.

Revenge – Someone said that "revenge is a dish best served cold" and I say how else could it be served? Now I must admit that taking revenge is one of my greatest temptations but I do resist. They say there's nothing like the sweet taste of revenge but they fail to mention the bitter after taste. The bible says in **Romans 12:17 thru 21;** Recompense to no man evil for evil. Provide things honest in the sight of all men.

If it be possible, as much as lieth in you, live peaceably with all men.

Dearly beloved, avenge not yourselves, but rather give place unto wrath: for it is written, **Vengeance** is mine; I will repay, saith the Lord.

Therefore if thine enemy hunger, feed him; if he thirst, give him drink: for in so doing thou shalt heap coals of fire on his head.

Be not overcome of evil, but overcome evil with good.

Also Matthew 5:38 – 39 states: Ye have heard that it hath been said, an eye for an eye, and a tooth for a tooth: But I say unto you, that ye resist not evil: but whosoever shall smite thee on thy right cheek, turn to him the other also.

Mahatma Gandhi said "an eye for an eye only ends up making the whole world blind." And Juvenal (the Roman poet active in the late 1st and early 2nd century CE, not to be confused with the rapper Juvenile) wrote "revenge is always the weak pleasure of a little and narrow mind."

Never the less it just seems to me that I should be the one to exact justice on the person who wronged me but I resist, and you should too!

SEX – Hee, hee, hee! Okay y'all know more about this than I do but these are random thoughts. I'm thinking about the revolution of sexuality and how things that were once taboo are now sooooooo acceptable. Take for example oral sex, not my cum of tea, I mean cup of tea, not my cup of tea but y'all is doing dat, *bwaaaaaaah*. I remember when it was called a "white girl thang". A black woman would rather die than put a penis in her mouth. But now! I know black girls who brag about how they can out suck a Hoover. Okay, so much for that, like I said before it's really not that kind of book.

So, is it right or wrong? I do have an answer for that question but y'all going to do what y'all going to do. I just want to know. What do y'all think of while you're doing it? Do you wash it first? Does it taste like chicken? *Bwaaaaaaaaaaaaaaaaaaaaaaaaaaaaah!!!!!!* I'm sorry but I just can't believe that somebody could put a penis in their mouth. Yuk, yuk, yuk. How can you put something in your mouth that is constantly contaminated by pee and dookey? And men you know the stuff that comes out of us, yet you'll stick your tongue… ilck.

So again, should you do it? Hum, I say no. But let me warn you, there is one kind of woman that can steal your man, that's the one that can really cook and give good head. I hope I didn't offend my church people but it's the truth and the Bible did say for the older sisters to teach the younger sisters. So again, should… you…do it? I still say no, ilck! That's un-naaaaaaa-tural.

Yes times sure have brought about a change. Now I'm getting up in age so I can say "I remember when". I remember when "good girls" pretended that they didn't want to have sex. Now they practically beg boys to "do it" to them. The so called good girl barely exists anymore. I hate that ladies have gotten so brazen and shameless but I'm glad that we don't have to pretend that we don't like sex. I used to hear women say that the reason they lost their virginity was because they were curious. I don't believe it. They lost their virginity because they were sexually aroused and that's all there is to it.

So how do we handle this revolution? How do we teach young ladies that it's not a shame to have these feelings without encouraging bad behavior? I don't know. Ask yo momma. I'm just an Auntie. *Tee-hee.*

Tattoos – I love tattoos! I know I'm not supposed to but hey I'm an artist. Some people say that it's desecrating the body but I don't see it. The same people who say that have their ears pierced. I think that everything should be done tastefully but I just can't say with a clear conscious that it's wrong. Okay, now that I got that out of the way, there is one tattoo that I don't believe in. I hate it when women tattoo their man's name on their bodies. This is one of the dumbest things you can do. Here you are married to Bob and you got Koran's name tattooed on your chest. You dummy! Come on ladies, it's time out for stupidity. Now you have to come up with a clever way to cover up this mistake. So here's a solution to fix some of the more common names.

If your ex's name was John just add Doe; if Clark add Kent; if Peter add Parker; if Billy add Goat; if Bob add Cat; if Donald add Duck and if Marvin add Gardens…*Bwaaaaaaah.* Well, you get the picture. The only acceptable name to tattoo on your body is Dick… ain't nothing wrong with Dick. Hee, hee, I'm sorry but my nieces would have expected me to say that.

Whores vs. Hoes – Yep, there's a difference. The bible speaks of whores but a hoe is a *whores* of a different color.

A whore is a person who engages in pre-marital sex. Anybody out there know any whores? In these modern days it seems to be perfectly acceptable to be a whore as long as you're not a hoe.

A hoe is classified as a woman who sleeps with a lot of different men. This is a dangerous woman. She has no restraint. She'll sleep with old men, young men, big men, little men, yo man, her sister's man and even her momma's man. Y'all look down your nose at these women and call them trash and you might be right. But even though we acknowledge that there's a difference between the whore and the hoe, God sees them as the same. So the next time you fix your lips to call somebody a hoe, you might just want to look in the mirror.

Chapter 18

That's Just Ghetto, Stop it!

Did you know that you could use CD cases for picture frames and that Kool-Aid makes a great substitute for temporary hair dye? Some might say that's just ghetto but being ghetto can be another way of being very creative.

We oft times interchange the word ghetto for tactless, tasteless, unintelligent, disingenuous or just plain stupid but actually it really means just the opposite. Being ghetto could actually be the same as being ingenuous.

Sometimes being ghetto is so funny but some things aren't. Some things are just tactless, tasteless, unintelligent and just plain stupid. These are the things we need to stop doing so let's just start off with an easy one and go on from there:

- Quit taking sugar, ketchup, straws, toilet paper and napkins from the fast food joints. Okay that's not so bad, it's just so ghetto. But the rest of these y'all have to stop!
- Quit running out of pads/tampons and using wads of tissue. You know you're going to have a period every month. Buy two boxes, when you open the second box it's time to buy another. It's okay to buy extra. They're not perishable. They won't spoil.
- Please buy dog food for your dog. People food is for people! If you can't afford dog food, you can't afford the dog.

- **Important**, cigarettes and crack cocaine are not diet aids. I know people who smoke to lose weight or won't quit because they don't want to gain weight. People! There's a better way.
- Stop telling the Welfare office that you and your husband are separated just to get food stamps.
- Stop giving people your kids' social security numbers so that they could claim them on their taxes, get more money back and split it with you. When they decide to use that social security number to steal your child's identity don't say a word.
- Stop washing out one pair of panties by hand and putting it in the dryer by itself while you're getting ready for work.
- Ladies stop telling your kids that every man you date is their uncle. Some of these poor kids have twenty uncles. And some of these Uncles are telling your kids to "come sit on Uncle's lap" while you're not looking.
- The only thing worse than telling your kids that your man is their uncle is telling them that he is their daddy. It's confusing when they have a different daddy every month.
- Mothers, stop putting perms in your two-year-old's hair. Yep, I know a woman who did it. The little girl just could walk. What did she need with a perm?
- Okay, ahhhhhhh, this one kills me. Stop telling your brilliant children to act stupid so they can get a SSI check. Some

of y'all even make your kids get bad grades in school just so you can keep a check. I know of a woman who told her child that he "bet" not know his abc's when they test him.

- Stop asking your kids to lie for you, i.e. tell the bill man I ain't home. *"My momma said her ain't home"* bwaaaaaaah! That's too much pressure on your kids. You can't even keep up with your own lies and when they mess up you have the nerve to get mad and want to kill them. Stop that ghetto mess.
- I love the way the young urban generation speaks. They have their own language. But please learn a little English. You'll need it to succeed in this world.
- Last but not least, if I've said it once I've said it a thousand times; black people, if you want your child to get a good job, stop giving them those made up names. I'm sorry. I know I'm going to get cussed out about this. But it's still true. So I beg your forgiveness from A to Z, Alberquanitha, Boomshika, Clamidia, Dafinest, Ejaculatia, Frankenstina, Gonakoreha, Hoeshia, Inkieralee, Ja'Darius, Kevonte, Laquanda, Manquinia, Nevaeh, Osendai, Pissonme, Quakconme, Reinonme, Snowonme, Testosteronia, Utherina, Vyce, Wyce, Xice (also spelled Zice), Yce, Zice (also spelled Xice). Of all these names Nevaeh is my favorite. That's Heaven spelled backwards. Hey! Ain't that Hell? *Bwaaaaaaah!* Wow.

Chapter 19

Twenty-one Questions

Every since we were children our parents, teachers or some other adult has asked us what we want to be when we grow up and as adults you've often heard the question "Where do you see yourself in five years, ten years or even fifteen years." Twelve year olds should see themselves graduating high school then college, trade school or some form of higher education. You're never too young to question yourself and it's never too soon to start making a life plan.

Life runs smoother when you have a plan.

To quote Robert Burns, "The best laid schemes o' mice an' men gang aft a-gley" **or as we love to misquote it:** The best laid plans of mice and men often go astray. So, should we stop planning? Well one of my other favorite quotes is "Fail to plan, plan to fail."

Don't go through life flying blind. Have a Plan-A, a Plan-B and a Back-up Plan. And remember it is okay to change your mind.

Here are 21 questions you may want to ask yourself while making out your life long plans:

What are your goals in life?

____

____

____

____

____

____

____

What must you do to reach your goals?

____

____

____

____

____

What do you consider your weaknesses?

____

____

____

____

____

What do you consider your strengths?

What do you dislike about your life that you can change?

What do you need to do to bring about this change?

What hinders you from bringing about this change?

What's the one thing about your life that you would never change?

What things in your life stress you most? (List them)

What most relieves your stress?

Who has the most positive influence over you?

____

Who has the most negative influence over you?

____

What do you love? (List them)

____

____

____

____

____

What do you hate? (List them).

____

____

____

____

____

When would you like to get married?

____

____

When would you like to start a family?

____

How would marriage or children affect your lifestyle?

How important is money to you?

What would be your ideal career if you could do anything?

Where would you live if you could live anywhere in the world?

What's one thing you would love to do before you die?

Chapter 20

So You Want to Get Married?

"Love maybe blind, but marriage is a real eye opener!" One of my nieces told me that. There has been some debate as to what is the best age to get married. Some folks believe that couples should wait until they're in their late twenties. They say that you should get an education, start your career and have a financially stable life before tying the knot. Many believe that teenagers should never be allowed to marry. Yet I personally know a lot of people that married in their teens, have been married for over twenty-five years and counting. But honestly the divorce rate for people who marry young I believe is over fifty percent.

So what is the right age to get married? I mean what is a good age? I say any age he asks you. Gurrrrrrrl take the chance if… you… want to. My point is you do what… you… want. Make your own decision. It's okay to listen to older folk's advice but in the end don't turn away a good man just because other people couldn't make their marriage work. And that line about missing out, trust, you're not missing out on anything. The only time I say you're too young to get married is if I have to sign for you. I mean if you're not old enough to sign for yourself are you really old enough to get married?

So, like most women, every since I was a little girl I've dreamed of my wedding. I've seen a lot of weddings growing up and I've picked up some valuable tips along the way. The dream has changed over years of time, the theme, the colors, the type of invitation, the type of cake and especially the groom…*bwaaaaaaah.* But there are some things that are fixed, some things you just can't get around and I have compiled a list.

I'll try to tell you the way it's traditionally supposed to be but as you well know in this day and time there are really no rules. Hopefully this chapter on wedding planning will be of help to you weather you're the bride, a friend of the bride, the mother of the bride or the coordinator. I'm not giving tips on personal things like the type of dress you should wear for the type of wedding you're having or the different kinds of wedding cakes available these days. You pick and decide on the wedding favors or table centerpieces. You won't find wedding theme ideals or honeymoon ideals in this chapter but the basics on how to get started planning your big day.

Your wedding is really "supposed to be" the way you want it. You may want it formal or informal, daytime or night. You may want to have a sit down reception or buffet style. I'll leave the details up to you. But there are many things that you may forget and this list may be a good guide for you. It is also a good ideal to make your own personal list adding those personal details.

I'm really going to try to stick to the basics and provide you with a few lists, followed by worksheets. Go ahead, fill in the blanks, be brave but write in pencil for you will usually want to change something.

List #1

Things to Buy/Rent

- Invitations
- Announcements
- Thank You Cards
- Stamps
- Programs purchased or made
- Unity candle
- Flower girl basket
- Bird seeds or Bubbles
- Ring pillow
- Garter
- Wedding favour
- Guestbook and pen set
- Cake knife and server
- Bride and Groom toast glasses
- Wedding Cake
- Wedding Cake topper
- Tablecloths
- Head table place set
- Dinnerware, Flatware and glasses
- Napkins and Matches
- Table centerpieces
- Decorations

- Limousine/transportation
- Archway
- Aisle Runner
- Kneeling Bench
- A Throw Away Bouquet
- Wishing well
- Flowers
- Liquor
- Special Gift for Matron of Honor
- Special Gift for Bestman
- Gifts for Bridesmaids
- Gifts for Groomsmen
- ____________________________
- ____________________________
- ____________________________
- ____________________________
- ____________________________
- ____________________________
- ____________________________
- ____________________________
- ____________________________
- ____________________________
- ____________________________
- ____________________________
- ____________________________

So who pays for what is the question. Over the years I have heard a lot of different answers to this question. So I'm going to give you one of the traditional guild lines to follow because I do like to hold to tradition.

Technically the wedding is the woman's and she has the "say so". That's the good news. The bad news is that the bride's family has the responsibility of paying for almost everything. So I'll tell you what the groom is responsible for (besides your rings). That makes it easier for me.

- Special Gift for Bestman
- Gifts for Groomsmen
- Flowers (now some disagree with me on this but the man should buy the flowers)
- Limousine/transportation
- Honeymoon

Those are the things that the groom pays for and well, the bride's family pays for everything else.

These are modern times and if traditional rules don't work for you break them. It is your wedding, make it work. When all else fails let the one with the money pay.

List #2

Things to Do

- Get Marriage License
- Send wedding announcement to newspaper
- Book the Church
- Compile a guest list
- Choose your Invitations

(include, Reply Cards, Reception Cards and Directions)

- Purchase gifts for bridal party
- Select Attendants
- Select Usher
- Select ceremony music
- Select Reception Hall
- Plan Dinner menu
- Plan Bar Drink Menu
- Choose your cake
- Choose your DJ
- Choose your guest favours
- Choose your flower
- Choose your photographer and videographer
- Change your Name

List #3

Important People
(You may need)

- Groom (hee hee)
- Coordinator
- Decorator
- Ushers
- DJ
- Bartender
- Attendant for gift table
- Head Hostess
- Doorman
- Reception Servers
- Florist
- Photographer
- Videographer
- Soloist
- Organist

Bride's name______________________

Groom's name________________________________

Wedding Date________________ Time ___________

Church or Facility _____________________________

Maid of Honor ________________________________

Matron of Honor ______________________________

Ushers 1.____________________________

2.____________________________

Bestman ______________________________________

Man of Distinction ____________________________

Bride's Maids:

1. ____

2. ____

3. ____

4. ____

5. ____

6. ____

7. ____

Groom's Men:

1. ____

2. ____

3. ____

4. ____

5. ____

6. ____

7. ____

Flower Girl ______________________________

Ring Barer ______________________________

Dress Designer ___________________________

Hair Stylist ______________________________

Officiator ________________________________

Ceremony Musician ________________________

Soloist 1.________________________________

Soloist 2.________________________________

Florist ___________________________________

Cake Designer ____________________________

Photographer______________________________

Videographer______________________________

DJ _______________________________________

Bartender ________________________________

Door Man ________________________________

Gift Table Attendant _____________________________

Coordinator_____________________________________

Reception Hall ___________________________________

Reception Hostess and Servers:

1. Hostess______________________________________
2. Server ______________________________________
3. Server ______________________________________
4. Server ______________________________________
5. Server ______________________________________
6. Server ______________________________________
7. Server ______________________________________

Menu

Drink Menu

Guest List Worksheet

1. ______________________________
2. ______________________________
3. ______________________________
4. ______________________________
5. ______________________________
6. ______________________________
7. ______________________________
8. ______________________________
9. ______________________________
10. ______________________________
11. ______________________________
12. ______________________________
13. ______________________________
14. ______________________________
15. ______________________________
16. ______________________________
17. ______________________________
18. ______________________________
19. ______________________________
20. ______________________________
21. ______________________________
22. ______________________________
23. ______________________________
24. ______________________________
25. ______________________________

26. ______________________________

27. ______________________________

28. ______________________________

29. ______________________________

30. ______________________________

31. ______________________________

32. ______________________________

33. ______________________________

34. ______________________________

35. ______________________________

36. ______________________________

37. ______________________________

38. ______________________________

39. ______________________________

40. ______________________________

41. ______________________________

42. ______________________________

43. ______________________________

44. ______________________________

45. ______________________________

46. ______________________________

47. ______________________________

48. ______________________________

49. ______________________________

50. ______________________________

51. ______________________________

52. ______________________________

53. ______________________________

54. ______________________________

55. ______________________________

56. ______________________________

57. ______________________________

58. ______________________________

59. ______________________________

60. ______________________________

61. ______________________________

62. ______________________________

63. ______________________________

64. ______________________________

65. ______________________________

66. ______________________________

67. ______________________________

68. ______________________________

69. ______________________________

70. ______________________________

71. ______________________________

72. ______________________________

73. ______________________________

74. ______________________________

75. ______________________________

76. ____

77. ____

78. ____

79. ____

80. ____

81. ____

82. ____

83. ____

84. ____

85. ____

86. ____

87. ____

88. ____

89. ____

90. ____

91. ____

92. ____

93. ____

94. ____

95. ____

96. ____

97. ____

98. ____

99. ____

100. ____

101.____

102.____

103.____

104.____

105.____

106.____

107.____

108.____

109.____

110.____

111.____

112.____

113.____

114.____

115.____

116.____

117.____

118.____

119.____

120.____

121.____

122.____

123.____

124.____

125.____

126.____

127.____

128.____

129.____

130.____

131.____

132.____

133.____

134.____

135.____

136.____

137.____

138.____

139.____

140.____

141.____

142.____

143.____

144.____

145.____

146.____

147.____

148.____

149.____

150.____

151.____

152.____

153.____

154.____

155.____

156.____

157.____

158.____

159.____

160.____

161.____

162.____

163.____

164.____

165.____

166.____

167.____

168.____

169.____

170.____

171.____

172.____

173.____

174.____

175.____

176.______________________________

177.______________________________

178.______________________________

179.______________________________

180.______________________________

181.______________________________

182.______________________________

183.______________________________

184.______________________________

185.______________________________

186.______________________________

187.______________________________

188.______________________________

189.______________________________

190.______________________________

191.______________________________

192.______________________________

193.______________________________

194.______________________________

195.______________________________

196.______________________________

197.______________________________

198.______________________________

199.______________________________

200.______________________________

Photographer's Checklist

- ❑ Bride
- ❑ Groom
- ❑ Bride and Groom
- ❑ Bride, Groom and Parents
- ❑ Bride, Groom and Her Parents
- ❑ Bride, Groom and His Parents
- ❑ Bride and Matron of Honor
- ❑ Bride with Attendants
- ❑ Groom and Bestman
- ❑ Groom with Attendants
- ❑ Groom and Bestman
- ❑ Wedding Party
- ❑ Flower Girl and Ring Bearer
- ❑ Clergy
- ❑ Musician
- ❑ Soloist
- ❑ Ushers
- ❑ Hostesses
- ❑ Rings
- ❑ Cake
- ❑ Cake Cutting

- ❑ Bouquet
- ❑ Bouquet Toss
- ❑ Garter removal
- ❑ Garter Toss
- ❑ Wishing Well

OTHERS

____
____
____
____
____
____
____
____
____
____
____
____
____
____
____
____
____

Notes:

(Write down your personalized notes of things you don't want to forget; i.e. wedding theme, special songs for wedding party entrance, garter removal, first and last dance etc.) I took the liberty of starting the list for you.

Something old Something new Something borrowed Something blue

Bride's Emergency Kit (pins, hair pins, extra pantyhose, lotion, comb etc)

A pair of comfy shoes for when you are ready to come out of those heels

Notes:

Notes:

Notes:

Notes:

Notes:

Notes:

Notes:

Notes:

Notes:

Notes:

Disclaimer

Before I wrote one word of this book I knew going in that I would have problems with some people in questionable authority, i.e. Doctors, Teachers, Clergymen, Psychiatrist and um, um.........................Mothers hee, hee, hee.

So let me just say this book was not written to impose my values on you or your family but to maybe encourage more dialogue between family members on their values.

All data and information provided in this book is for informational purposes only including hints, tips and home remedies. I make no representations as to accuracy, completeness, suitability, or validity of any information in this book and will not be liable for any losses, injuries, or damages arising from its display or use. Some stories are based on actual events. In certain cases incidents, characters and timelines have been changed for dramatic purposes. Certain characters may be composites, or entirely fictitious in which case any similarity to any person living or dead is merely coincidental.

Coming Soon

You won't want to miss the companion issue to Bad Auntie, "Bad Auntie, Letters to My Nephews". There have been things that my nephews have asked me but mostly there are things that I wish they had.

In this companion book I will cover issues like: Job Hunting, Men's Health, Black Women vs. White Women and Dirty Tricks Women Play

If you've enjoyed Bad Auntie you must read its companion book "Bad Auntie, Letters to My Nephews".

To all my supporters,

I want to tell you about Magnificent Images' Scholarship program.

The ***Julius Gore I Memorial scholarship*** is a scholarship awarded to graduating high school students with a grade point average **between 2.5 and 3.0** with an outstanding disposition and an immense desire to further their education. This Scholarship is aimed towards dedicated and intelligent individuals that are often overlooked. Many students who do not achieve high GPA's go on to become college graduates while other's with superior GPA's fail. Theses students are rarely offered scholarships or grants of any kind. The ***Julius Gore I Memorial scholarships*** are offered only to these individuals. Many students in High School receive grades that don't truly reflect their intelligence. For example, I went to High School with a girl who received mostly D's on her report card. She went on to college and made the Dean's list repeatedly. She is now a very successful highly paid executive.

The winner of this scholarship must however prove that they are deserving of this award. They will be scrutinized very closely and must complete an application plus all other requirements including an essay.

In contrast, the ***Vickie Gore Collier Memorial Scholarship*** will be awarded to a college student who has completed their freshmen year with a grade point average of 3.0 or higher. A high GPA is necessary to receive this award and this student must have completed their first year of college.

Students need our help. I had a friend drop out of college after completing her freshman year because after paying her tuition and her room and board for her sophomore year, she could not afford her books. I went with her mother to pick her up. She had to pay back all student loans without ever receiving a degree and this sickened me.

I am seeking donors and I sincerely appreciate any donation you are able to offer, please remember that any amount helps! If you think that you can't afford to donate, send just one dollar. Dollar bills really add up. All checks and money orders should be made payable to Magnificent Images and sent to:

Magnificent Images
PO Box 10545
Erie, PA 16514

Please feel free to contact me at badauntie@yahoo.com if you have any questions regarding these Scholarships. Thank you for your consideration. With your help, I know we will succeed. Please use the scholarship donation form provided, and mail your donation to the address above. If you are missing the donation form, just write your name, address and gift amount on any slip of paper and mail it in along with your contribution.

Thank you for your support

Sincerely,

Rose M. Gore

Magnificent Images

Magnificent Images' Scholarships Fund Drive Scholarship

Donation form

Name______________________________________

Address____________________________________

City _________________________State__________

Email _________________________

Enclosed is a contribution for $_____________________

Thank you for your support

Please mail completed form along with your contribution to:

Magnificent Images

PO Box 10545

Erie, PA 16514

APPLICATION (page1)

Applications for the ***Julius Gore I Memorial Scholarship*** and the ***Vickie Gore Collier Memorial Scholarship*** will be accepted from high school seniors and college sophomores.

The scholarships are cash awards. (Winners must enter as full-time students).

Criteria:

First preference to Erie, PA resident

Please print clearly. Use extra paper if necessary.

Name

____Age______

Address____

City____________________________ State______

Zip____________

Phone

(______)____

Email address

____

APPLICATION (page 2)

College ____________________ 1^{St} year GPA________

(if applying for the Vickie Gore Collier Memorial Scholarship)

High School______________________ Grad Date_________

(if applying for the Julius Gore I Memorial scholarship)

Yearly Household Income_______________

Number of Dependents______

Employer__________________________

Address____

Have you decided yet on a college or university? ______

If yes, please give the name and location

____

Have You Applied for Admission? _____yes _____no

Educational Goal: _____Associate Degree_____Bachelor Degree

_____Masters Degree _____Doctoral

Subjects of interest or Major

____

____

My signature below certifies that I have received, read and understood all the rules and requirements of an applicant for the Magnificent Images Scholarships and that I meet all eligibility requirements.

Applicant's Signature

____________________________Date__________

APPLICATION (page3)

Rules

Write a personal statement about yourself, your educational and vocational goals. Please answer any or all of the following questions in a statement that is typed or printed, double-spaced, and **not to exceed three pages**.

- How have you contributed to your community?
- What hardships have you endured?
- Who has inspired you?
- Whom have you helped?
- What achievements are you proud of?
- Please list any awards or recognition you have received.
- What are your career and/or educational goals?

Please return completed application to:

Magnificent Images

P.O. Bx10545

Erie, PA 16514

About the Author

Rose M. Gore is an award winning Writer as well as a dynamic Graphics and Photo Media Professional. Many in the entertainment industry have sought Rose out for her impressive writing skills.

Miss Gore also has substantial experience in studio and freelance photography, commercial media art and graphic design. Her expertise runs the entire range - from as intricate as a music CD insert to as grandiose as an entire street scene on the interior walls of a school classroom.

Rose's photography engagements have included standard studio sittings; intimate/discreet sittings; and specialty shoots for actors, models, musicians and event shootings, such as the stage play "Ain't No Sunshine When He's Home, starring Cuba Gooding Sr., Sean Levert, Todd Bridges and Clyde R. Jones. Her conventional art services have included custom oil paintings; pencil sketches; abstract creations; caricatures; and scenic wall murals. Her graphic art services have included promotional flyers for actors, rappers and rock bands; direct mail pieces for charity fundraisers; CD inserts for various musicians and rap groups; company business directories and book cover designs

Miss Gore's designs have been placed on file with several Institutions including the Cedric The Entertainer Charitable Foundation. She has been asked to design graphics for many in the industry such as Omar Epps (BKNYC Records), Yvette Wilson (Fat Daddy records) and Juelz Santana's, Santana's Town clothing line.

Rose is the forth of five children born and raised in Erie, PA. Family is the most essential thing in Rose's life. Her Scholarship awards, dedicated to the memory of her late brother and sister are her most important projects.

CPSIA information can be obtained at www.ICGtesting.com
Printed in the USA
LVOW09s0555221014

409819LV00035BA/1640/P

9 781441 494498